MAK

B

MAKING DESIGNER

Bead & Wire Jewellery

Inspiring Techniques for Unique Designs

Tammy Powley

Published in the UK in 2005 by
Apple Press
Sheridan House
112/116A Western Road
Hove BN3 1DD
UK

www.apple-press.com

ISBN 1-84543-029-8

10 9 8 7 6 5 4 3 2 1

Design: Terry Patton Rhoads
All photos by Allan Penn
Illustrations by Judy Love

Printed in Singapore

CONTENTS

INTRODUCTION

Wire is one of the most versatile components used in jewelry making, and when combined with beads, the design possibilities dramatically increase. Common wire and bead techniques, such as making a bead and wire chain or threading wire through a single bead to make a bead-dangle, are usually part of the average jewelry designer's repertoire. However, you don't need to stop there; wire can allow you to do much more when it comes to expanding your jewelry-making skills. Creating wire findings, including ear hooks, headpins, and clasps, is one way to add another layer to your jewelry art, often enabling you to make each component of your finished piece.

Although the instructions in this book are intended to increase your potential for producing signature jewelry elements, all levels of jewelry makers, from the inexperienced beginner to the more seasoned craftperson, will find it a valuable resource. If you have never worked with beads or wire, don't be intimidated by the potential of creating each component. With practice and guidance from the projects in this book, you'll be amazed at what you can accomplish. For those who have already made numerous pieces of jewelry, you too will find inspiration and new ideas to broaden your abilities.

One reason for this book's wide range of design options is the generous techniques section, which provides step-by-step, illustrated instructions covering basic finishing methods along with detailed directions on using wire to construct your own findings. Building on the techniques section, the projects in this book offer you specific examples to follow so that you can then combine these methods and create unique pieces of finished jewelry. Throughout, you'll receive helpful jewelers' tips and design advice to assist you in constructing quality jewelry you will be proud to wear and give as gifts. Finally, each jewelry project also includes a variation, demonstrating alternative designs using the same basic elements. As you learn to master the techniques, you'll soon realize that each works as a continuation of the next, ultimately building your skill level until you are soon comfortable making every piece of your design.

ABOUT BEADS

If you already make beaded jewelry, then you are probably familiar with the addictive nature of beads. For those uninitiated into the world of beads, prepare yourself. One bead purchase inevitably leads to the next, and the next, and so on, until you find that you've become a bead-a-holic. However, the good news is that because there are so many types of beads available, they can inspire you to create a plethora of designs, from the classic to the exotic.

Although the huge variety of available beads can be daunting, it can be exciting as well. Beads are not just ornamental objects; they are significant artifacts that share a rich history throughout time, and you instantly become part of this history with the allocation of your first bead.

TYPES OF BEADS

Just about any item with a hole in it is a possible bead. Therefore, to attempt to list and describe every type of bead in existence would require more than just a few pages of text. Following is a list and brief description of some of the most common types of beads used for designing jewelry.

Gemstones

Extremely popular, gemstone beads come in a large variety of stones, shapes, and sizes.

Precious: Rubies, emeralds, sapphires, and diamonds are called "precious" gemstones because of their limited availability. Although you most often see precious gemstones used in fine jewelry, such as diamond rings and ruby ear studs, these stones are also available in the form of beads. As you can imagine, the price for precious gemstone beads is comparative to their fine jewelry relatives. However, imagine a beautiful necklace made with ruby beads!

Semiprecious: Because these stones are more readily available than precious gemstones, they are also more affordable. They come in a wide variety of stones, from agate to zoizite. Most beaders are big fans of semiprecious gemstone beads because they allow you to create high-quality jewelry using natural elements from the earth. If you are a lover of stone beads, make sure you take a look at my book *Making Designer Gemstone and Pearl Jewelry* for more information about gemstones and how to use them in your jewelry creations.

Organic: Although they are not made of stone, organic beads, such as pearls and amber, are sometimes included under the gemstone category. For more information on organic beads, refer to the Natural Materials section.

Natural Materials

Along with gemstones, there are many other naturally occurring materials used in beading.

Pearls: An organic element, pearls are classics when it comes to jewelry making. They occur in nature when a foreign object finds its way into an oyster. The oyster then tries to protect itself by forming layers of what eventually becomes the pearl over the foreign matter. Today, pearl farmers use nature combined with science to grow and then harvest pearls. There are salt water and freshwater varieties, but the latter are more popular because they are more affordable and come in a large selection of colors, shapes, and sizes.

Coral: Like pearls, coral grows naturally in water; specifically, it is the skeletal remains of past sea life. For centuries, coral has been a fashionable form of ornamentation. Its popularity, combined with other factors, such as pollution, however, has resulted in a struggle for survival for coral reefs, which are the natural habitat for many species of sea life. There are some legal harvesters of coral, but there are also many who are indiscriminately damaging this important natural resource. Therefore, many jewelry makers choose to use faux coral for their designs. Normally made of glass or resin, imitation coral gives you the glamour of coral without the possible guilt.

Shell: Available in whole pieces or in parts, shell beads are beautiful tributes to nature. Some of the more common shell beads are mother-of-pearl, paua, and trocha. Mother-of-pearl is very popular and comes in lots of different shapes. It is available in its natural color, a sort of creamy mixture of beiges, or in pure white, which is created using a bleaching process.

Amber: The Romans called amber *succinum*, which is Latin for "juice." This organic gem comes from preserved tree resin, sometimes dating back tens of millions of years. Its basic orange color ranges from dark honey to reddish orange to hazy lemon. Extremely large pieces of amber are rare, and some vendors weigh these chunks of amber to determine the price so that the purchaser pays by the gram. Although it really depends on your preference, darker amber is usually a little more expensive than lighter amber.

Bone: Probably the most ancient of all bead types are bone beads. It's not too difficult to envision ancient humans wearing necklaces made from bones and leather. Today, bone beads are available in a large selection of shapes, and many include patterns carved into their surface. Most bone beads sold today are made of ox or cow bone.

Wood: Beads carved from wood are not as popular as they were during the '60s and '70s, when they were used in macramé jewelry, but they are still available from many beading suppliers. These are especially useful in jewelry that uses thicker stringing material, such as leather, waxed linen, or hemp, and though they come in an assortment of colors, the natural hues of browns and blacks are probably what most people envision when they think about beads made of wood.

Crystals

Vying for popularity next to gemstones, crystal beads are just about essential for anyone making wire and bead jewelry.

Czech: As the name implies, these crystals come from the Czech Republic, but most beaders shorten the name to "Czech" when referring to these crystal beads. These beads are machine cut, creating highly faceted beads that normally range in size from as small as 3 mm to as large as 8 mm. The most common shapes are round, bicone, and teardrop, and the available colors for Czech beads are extensive. Most colors also come in an aurora borealis finish, referred to as AB, which creates an almost mirror effect. These crystals are considered midgrade quality and are, therefore, very economical for jewelry designers.

Austrian: Crystal beads from Austria are primarily manufactured today by Swarovski, a company that is well-known for innovation in the lead crystal industry. In the late nineteenth century, Daniel Swarovski developed a new method for cutting crystals, and though the company makes a large number of products, their crystal beads have become essential jewelry components in the world of beading for those who love sparkle. These are the "Cadillacs of crystals," and their price range reflects the high quality and brilliance of these precisely cut, luxurious beads.

Vintage: The label "vintage" can be very misleading when it comes to beads and fashion in general. Although we'd like to believe it refers to items an elderly Victorian matriarch might wear, in reality, vintage can refer to anything, especially beads manufactured after World War I up to the 1970s. Some crystal vendors specialize in vintage beads, and though they can be made of many different materials, crystals are the most sought after.

Antique: Generally, anything over 100 years old is considered an antique, but when it comes to beads, most notably crystal beads, this succinct definition begins to blur because this is a topic of controversy among beaders. Because "vintage" crystals date after World War I, antique crystals obviously predate this, right? To a certain extent, this is true. However, other considerations are important, such as the cut and color of the crystals; when manufacturers stop making a certain type of crystal, these discontinued beads are sometimes awarded the status of "antique." Therefore, it is important for crystal bead connoisseurs to educate themselves about the different cuts and colors of crystals so they can distinguish between "vintage" and "antique."

Glass

Beads made of glass come in a large assortment and, depending on the type, are either man- or machine-made.

Lampwork: If you've ever had the opportunity to watch a lampwork artist at work, or even tried to make these beads yourself, then you will have instantaneous appreciation for the skill and workmanship that goes into making lampwork beads. The name comes from the fact that the artist works over an open flame with a glass rod in one hand and a metal rod, known as a bead mandrel, in the other. As the flame heats the glass, the lampworker allows the glass to run down onto the mandrel while she simultaneously rotates the mandrel to create a bead. Once a lampworker is finished creating her bead, she then anneals it, which is a slow cooling process ordinarily requiring that the bead be placed in a low-temperature kiln. Lampwork beads must cool slowly to maintain the integrity of the glass. Otherwise, they will shatter and break.

Furnace glass: The technique for making furnace glass beads, also sometimes known as cane beads, is similar to lampwork because it uses heat. The difference is that the glass for these beads is heated using a furnace, just as glass blowers use a furnace to make glass vases and bowls. Cane makers create long, hollow canes of glass that they then cut up to create beads. Colors and shapes vary, but you'll usually find these beads are clear with streaks of color throughout and are formed in a diverse number of geometric shapes.

Pressed glass: Whereas the technique for making lampwork beads is similar to that of blown glass, pressed glass is formed by pouring hot glass into molds and pressing it, thus conforming to the mold. Some pressed glass beads may almost look like lampwork beads, but they are less expensive because the procedure for making them is faster and thus allows for larger quantities. India produces most of the pressed glass beads used in jewelry making, and the variety of colors, sizes, and shapes is quite large. As with most beads, though, round seems to be forever popular; however, you can also buy pressed glass beads in the shape of leaves, hearts, flowers, stars, teardrops, and even fish.

Seed: Tiny seed beads are important elements for a form of jewelry known as bead weaving. Jewelry makers, or bead weavers, use techniques where they stitch the beads together to form a tremendous array of designs. The majority of the stitches used in seed beading, such as peyote, come from ancient civilizations, including Native Americans and tribes from South Africa. The beads used today primarily come from the Czech Republic and Japan. Although Czech seed beads [see page 16] have brilliant colors and are the least expensive, Japanese seed beads are more precisely cut. The results are beads that allow for an even and uniform weave. In fact, the Japanese are responsible for an extremely precise cut of seed bead known as a Delica, which is very popular for the peyote stitch because the beads can sit so closely together that the effect is similar to stacks of tiny bricks.

Clay

Clay beads are another form of handcrated beads, and they continue to grow in popularity.

Polymer clay: In jewelry-making circles, polymer clay goes by the acronym PC. This clay is available at most craft stores and comes in an array of colors. PC artists first condition and then hand-shape the clay into beads. Conditioning requires that they fold and press the clay to make it soft, a technique so similar to working with dough that PC artists use pasta machines to help roll the clay. This gives it elasticity and makes the next steps of rolling, shaping, and cutting beads easier. After they shape their beads, they must then bake the clay in a conventional oven. Finally, some PC artists take additional steps of sanding and then coating their beads with a sealant to protect the beads from cracking or breaking.

Metal clay: The words "metal" and "clay" don't seem like they go together, but metal clay beads are some of the fastest growing forms of bead making today. Many of the properties of metal clay and polymer clay are the same, but metal clay must be baked in a kiln or fired with a torch. After the heating process is finished, the end result is a metal bead. This unique clay material is available in both gold and fine silver.

Metal

Whether they are made of gold, silver, copper, brass, or pewter, metal beads are great to use as accent beads and to mix with gemstone and crystal beads.

Plated: Metal beads are sometimes plated, most often with sterling silver or gold. Silver beads are also sometimes plated with gold. A few terms you may already be familiar with include vermeil and electroplating. The plating allows for the look of a higher-end bead at a lower cost. Some beads are plated better than others, but inevitably the plating can wear off or become discolored. For some beads, such as gold vermeil, this look can create a patina appearance and enhance the piece as it ages; for others, such as resin beads, the plating can chip off and the resin will show through.

Base: Any metals that are not precious metals (silver, gold, and platinum) are referred to as base metals. These include copper, aluminum, nickel, and steel. For example, many findings (ear hooks, bead tips, and clasps) are available in surgical steel. Beads are also available in base metal, with copper being the most popular; beads made of nickel are normally plated with silver or gold.

Cast: The majority of metal beads are created using a method called lost wax casting. The initial bead begins as a wax mold. Then a jeweler inserts the molds into a metal flask, pours a plaster substance inside of it, and heats the flask until the wax melts, leaving a hardened impression of the bead inside the plaster. Finally, centrifugal force is used to pour hot metal (such as gold or silver) into the impression. The jeweler quenches the heated flask, and then removes the plaster to reveal the metal beads. This casting process enables jewelers to make multiple beads relatively quickly.

Bali-style: Bali, Indonesia, is well known for its skilled metal artisans. For metal bead enthusiasts, Bali beads are at the top of the list when it comes to quality and fine craftsmanship. These artists use silversmithing techniques, including granulation, appliqué, and etching, to handcraft each bead individually. Because of the popularity of these beads, the Bali legacy has inspired numerous knockoff beads over the last few years, referred to as "Bali-style" beads. Proponents of Bali beads will argue that there is no comparison as far as quality, but both bead types are excellent additions to your jewelry designs if you like to add an ethnic flare.

BUYING BEADS

Locating beads, understanding how they are sold and packaged, and then determining the best deals and bead quality are important considerations when you purchase beads. Jewelry making has grown into a huge market, and for the beginner, it can be overwhelming when you walk into your first bead store or cruise the Internet reading about hanks and kilos. As you become integrated into the beading world, you'll soon feel comfortable. The information below will help you sort out all this information and make educated purchases.

Bead Suppliers

No matter what your bead preferences are, from tiny glass seed beads to earthy gemstone beads, there's a bead supplier for you. The larger bead vendors import much of their inventory from around the world, and lots of smaller suppliers specialize in particular types of beads to fill a marketplace niche. With so many options for jewelry makers, it's not difficult to find the beading supplies you need. For a specific list, refer to the Suppliers section on page 122.

Bead shops: Veteran as well as novice jewelry makers will find plenty to tempt them in a bead shop. Even though retail bead shops may charge a little more than other venues, nothing beats the tactile experience of hand picking your beads and the helpful one-on-one attention that a bead shop offers. The average bead shop is privately owned and operated by people who love beads just as much as you do. They also offer jewelry-making classes, so they are a good place for beginners to get started. To find a bead shop near you, check your local *Yellow Pages* and classified ads in bead and jewelry-making magazines.

Catalogs: Large and midsize suppliers will sometimes have a catalog available and may send out sales fliers and supplements on occasion. Depending on the size of the catalog, these can be really useful when learning your craft because they allow you to compare different types of tools, equipment, and of course, beads. Although you can't actually touch the beads, browsing through a catalog is an enjoyable way to shop, and some suppliers offer discounts for bulk purchases. One disadvantage, however, is the fact that most catalog merchants charge for shipping and handling. This is important to keep in mind, and if possible, you may want to team up with a few bead buddies on one order to help cut down on these extra costs.

Online: The Internet has revolutionized more than one industry, including jewelry making. Web stores have allowed larger companies to display their inventory online, and small one-person operations can just about compete with them due to the low cost and easy access of starting a Web business. Along with Web-based companies, Internet auction sites are another popular place to buy beads and related supplies. The best part of buying online is convenience. You can literally shop by pressing a few buttons and clicking away with your mouse. The disadvantages are similar to those of catalog shopping. You will probably get charged for shipping and handling, and you don't actually get to see your merchandise until it arrives at your door. Another important consideration, most notably for auctions, is to be aware of current price trends. Just because an item is up for auction doesn't mean it's always a good deal, and sometimes a hefty shipping charge is added to your final bid. Read the fine print before you bid on any item.

Bead shows: Like a bead shop, bead and gem shows allow you to touch the merchandise before you decide to buy. Somewhat like an art show, bead shows are organized by companies who get a group of bead vendors together to sell their beads and related supplies. Vendors pay for booth space, and buyers come to shop. Along with the advantage of seeing the beads, most shows offer a large variety of merchandise and some bead sellers will offer quantity discounts. The downside is that they normally charge an entrance fee to buyers and you may have to drive a good distance to get to one. To find out whether there are any bead shows coming to your local area, scan the ads in bead- and jewelry-related magazines for a list of schedules and locations.

Craft stores: The surging growth of the jewelry-making industry has not gone unnoticed by craft stores. Large craft stores, especially chain stores, now carry a huge variety of beads and related supplies. At one time, the quality of beads at craft stores was low to medium at best, but this has changed. Craft stores now carry an assortment from low-end wooden beads to higher-end crystals. Unlike bead stores that allow you to buy per bead, however, most craft stores sell their beads in small packages. Their prices are also sometimes a little higher than other suppliers, which is probably due to their large overhead. Another drawback is that they may not have staff knowledgeable enough about jewelry making to help you because they sell supplies for other types of arts and crafts, not just jewelry making.

Bead Packaging

When you start buying beads, you'll soon realize that they come in all sorts of quantities and, for the most part, are packaged according to bead type.

Hanks (A): Czech seed beads are sold by the hank, which means they are temporarily strung on nylon or silk cord with sometimes as many as ten or twelve strings of beads per hank. Although the number of beads per hank depends on the size of the beads, the average-size 11 hank of seed beads has approximately 4,000 beads on it.

Unfinished strands (B): Gemstones, pearls, and sometimes crystal beads come temporarily strung on nylon or monofilament which is tied at the end, sort of like a necklace without a clasp. Lengths can vary, but the average length of these strands is 16" (40 cm). The number of beads per strand depends on the length as well as the diameter of the beads.

Continuous strands (C): Gemstone beads in the form of chips, also referred to as nuggets, are normally purchased on 36" (90 cm) continuous strands. The knot that connects one end to the other is difficult to find sometimes, so you can wear these long necklaces as they are, though most jewelry makers cut them up and incorporate the chipped beads into their jewelry designs.

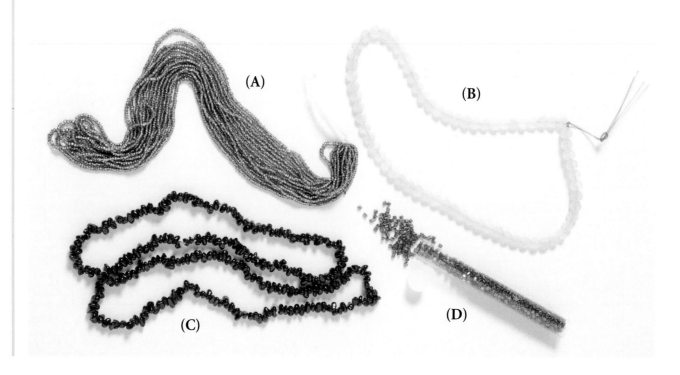

(A)

(B)

(C)

(D)

Tubes (D): Japanese seed beads and Japanese Delica beads are sold by the gram and come in clear plastic tubes. Because Delicas are a little more expensive than regular seed beads, the tubes are usually sold in smaller amounts, about 10 grams per tube. Regular Japanese seed beads are usually sold in 30-gram tubes. This can vary, however, because many vendors buy seed beads by the kilo and then split them up into smaller portions for retail purposes.

Kilos: The serious seed beader who needs a lot of beads or who decides to start retailing seed beads, will have to buy her Japanese seed beads by the kilo or half kilo.

Grams: Along with seed beads, suppliers also sell many metal beads, such as Bali beads and pressed-glass beads by the gram. This means that they have a fixed price (for example, thirty-five cents per gram) and retailers will weigh a bead before they sell it to you. The amount they charge per gram is important to know when you are shopping around and comparing prices.

Pounds: Although some bead shops will sell furnace glass (also referred to as cane beads) individually, if you want to buy more than one bead at a time, most vendors charge a price per pound for these. Pressed-glass and lower-end lampwork beads (usually imported from India) are also sold in bulk by the pound.

Gross: One gross is equal to 144 pieces. If you buy beads or findings in quantity, you'll probably see some suppliers who sell them packaged in gross or half-gross quantities.

Prepackaged: Vendors can prepackage beads just about any way they want, and the number of beads per package depends on the whim of the person selling them. When you see beads advertised as "sold per package," always double-check to see how many beads are included in each one so you are clear about the cost of each bead.

Individually: Purchasing beads individually can be difficult for suppliers who use catalogs or the Internet to sell their merchandise. However, bead shops are able to accommodate the "by the bead" buyer. This means you may lose out on any quantity discounts, but it also means you can buy exactly what you want, even if you just need a handful of beads to make one piece of jewelry.

Bead Purchasing Tips

There's no wrong way to shop for beads. Once you've visited a few bead shops and acquired a number of catalogs, you'll start to become more bead savvy, but here are a few tips to help make shopping more pleasurable.

- When buying beading supplies through the Internet or via a catalog, first check each vendor's shipping information. Additional costs for shipping, handling, and, in some cases, a restocking fee for returned merchandise are important considerations to be aware of before you make a purchase.

- Be flexible when traveling to shop for your beads. Most bead shops and shows have a constant influx of new inventory, so be prepared to find something you didn't expect.

- Make a list of those "must-have" items. Often, it can be overwhelming when you shop for beads, and you might get sidetracked and forget about the beads and related supplies that prompted you to go bead shopping in the first place.

- Most gemstones are dyed or treated in some way to enhance their color. This is a common practice in the industry, but it is important for you to know what you're getting. Vendors normally know what they are selling, but if not, look for clues, such as descriptive words added to the name of a bead strand. Some examples are "cape amethyst" instead of just "amethyst" or "stabilized turquoise" instead of just "turquoise."

- It's always nice to buy wholesale if possible, but be careful about applying for a state tax identification number just so you can do this. Although it will allow you to purchase from some wholesale distributors, there are a lot of other legal requirements that go along with it. Some vendors will sell wholesale to the public, so you may not need a tax number if you plan to keep your jewelry making as a hobby.

- Be aware of the size and quality of the holes in your beads. Smaller holes, such as those in pearl beads, need thinner wire and stringing material. Also, look at the way unfinished strands of beads lay on the strand. Are the beads lined up one behind the other? If not, this means that some of the holes are off center. Another quality check is to look at some of the holes to make sure there are no cracks in the beads around the holes. This is especially important for gemstone beads.

- Once your bead addiction kicks in, you'll discover that you will never have enough. This is when it's important to find other local beaders in your area so that you can team up and buy in bulk. Many vendors will give you price breaks for large quantities, and this will also help you save on shipping costs.

ABOUT WIRE

When working with wire for the first time, it is not unusual to make mistakes and have piles of deformed wire pieces. Therefore, it's always a good idea to use practice wire when learning new designs. Size 18-gauge (1 mm) copper wire is a good choice to practice with because it is inexpensive and can be purchased at some hardware stores. It is also available from wire suppliers. Once you are comfortable with a design, then you can choose from the wide variety of wire available on the market. (See the Suppliers section on page 122)

When selecting wire for a project, you need to make a few decisions. The size, type, hardness, and shape of your wire will make a difference in your finished product.

SIZES OF WIRE

When purchasing wire for your projects, it is important to understand how wire is sized. A wire's size is determined by its diameter. In North America, wire size is measured in gauge, and in most European countries, wire size is measured in millimeters. When selecting the correct gauge of wire, it is helpful to remember that the smaller the gauge number, the thicker the wire. Therefore, size 14-gauge (1.6 mm) is thicker than size 24-gauge (.5 mm).

The size of wire you use for a project will vary depending on your preference and what you plan to do with the wire. For example, a clasp needs to be stronger than an ear hook. So, you would probably want a thicker gauge wire for a clasp than you would for an ear hook. For a fixed gauge, copper is generally softer than silver, which, in turn, is softer than the same gauge of gold wire.

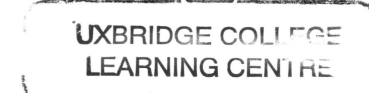

TYPES OF WIRE

Experimentation is always the best way to determine which type of wire works best for your needs, and there are many options available for today's jewelry artists.

Copper (A)

This is good to use as practice wire, but it also looks nice with some designs, such as those that incorporate earth tones.

Galvanized (B)

A dull silver color, this is also good practice wire and is often available at hardware stores.

Sterling Silver (C)

Sterling indicates that the wire is 92.5 percent pure silver. The rest is made up of metal alloys to provide strength.

Fine Silver (not shown)

Made of 99.9 percent pure silver, fine silver is softer than sterling, and because it has fewer alloys, it does not tarnish as quickly as sterling silver does.

Gold-filled (D)

If you like the look of gold but not the price, then you will like gold-filled wire, which has many layers of gold. It is not plated (only one layer), so gold-filled lasts for a long time if cared for properly.

Gold (not shown)

Once you've built up your confidence level, you can use real gold wire to create your findings. This wire is available in various karats (10 to 24, for example) and even different colors (such as rose gold and white gold).

Coated Colors (E)

Colored wire has become very popular and is even available in many large craft stores. It is a lot of fun to work with, but it's important to keep in mind that the wire is coated. If you aren't careful, you can mark the wire when using metal tools.

(A)

(B)

(C)

(D)

(E)

HARDNESS OF WIRE

When you are ready to purchase silver or gold-filled wire, you will notice that suppliers refer to the wire's hardness (dead soft, half-hard, and full-hard) as well as the size and type of wire when they list it in their catalogs. Wire manufacturers harden wire by pulling it through a draw plate (a tool with holes in it the same size and shape of the wire). The more times they pull the wire, the harder it becomes, and each type has its purpose.

Dead Soft: As the term indicates, this wire is very soft and you can easily bend it with your hands. Jewelry artists who specialize in a technique called wire sculpture often use dead-soft wire.

Half-Hard: Harder than dead-soft wire, half-hard wire is one of the most versatile because it is strong but still fairly easy to manipulate. Half-hard wire is used for the projects in this book.

Full-Hard: Wire wrap artists, who create jewelry by wrapping wires together rather than soldering wire, frequently prefer to use full-hard wire.

SHAPES OF WIRE

Wire is available in various shapes, such as round, half-round, and square. For the projects in this book, I have used round. However, you can create a slightly different look for your finished findings simply by changing the shape of the wire you use.

BASIC TOOL KIT

Just like a woodworker or mechanic, jewelry makers never have enough tools. If you are just starting, you don't need a toolbox full of tools, but you will need a few. Below is list of tools needed for the projects in this book. Make sure you have them available when you start working through the projects. This is by no means a complete list of tools. It is simply a place to start.

- Wire Cutters

- Flat or Bent-nosed Pliers

- Round-nosed Pliers

- Jewelers' Files

- Crimping Pliers

- Beading Awl

- Nylon-nosed Pliers

- Polishing Cloth

- Pencil

- Ruler

- Jewelers' Glue

Wire Cutters

A pair of flush-cut wire cutters will help ensure an even end to your wire when you cut it.

Flat- or Bent-nosed Pliers

Whether you use a flat- or bent-nosed pair of pliers is a personal choice. They will both help you accomplish the same task. Either way, they should be smooth on the inside of the nose and not textured. Flat-nosed pliers are sometimes also referred to as chain-nosed pliers.

Round-nosed Pliers

These are invaluable for making loops in your wire. They are made specifically for jewelry making, and most jewelry suppliers and many craft stores carry them.

Jewelers' Files

These usually come in a set of ten to twelve files and are very useful for making sure the ends of your wires are smooth.

Crimping Pliers

These pliers are designed specifically for attaching crimp beads. Some jewelry makers simply flatten crimp beads using flat-nosed pliers, but crimping pliers curl and then flatten the beads, creating a more professional finish.

Beading Awl

Used for knotting, this is a very basic tool consisting of a long, pointed piece of metal connected to a wooden handle. It helps you guide knots so they are securely positioned against your beads. In a pinch, you can also try using a corsage pin to accomplish the same task.

Nylon-nosed Pliers

These help you flatten wire without marking the wire. They are used for some of the projects in this book. You could use a pair of flat-nosed pliers and just cover the inside of the nose with a soft cloth so you don't make marks on the wire, but once you get serious about using wire in your jewelry designs, you will want to purchase a pair of these.

Polishing Cloth

A soft polishing cloth is useful for cleaning tarnished wire.

Pencil

A simple pencil is a handy tool for making large loops.

Ruler

You will need a ruler to measure pieces of wire.

Jewelers' Glue

Glues, also referred to as jewelers' cement, is used to set knots in nylon and silk cord.

WigJig® Olympus
Patent 6,253,798
www.wigjig.com (800) 579-WIRE

A wire jig is a possible alternative to using hand tools for making wire findings and other components.

USING A JIG

The more wire and bead jewelry you make, the more tools you will find yourself collecting. Personal preference will invariably dictate your choice of tools, and this includes the decision to use a specialized tool called a jig. Although there are a number of jig manufacturers and different jig models, the basic jig design resembles a pegboard. Rather than wrapping your wire around round-nosed pliers, you wrap wire round the pegs of the jig. Some jig models have stationary pegs, but many jigs are designed to allow wire workers to remove and rearrange the pegs into different formations or patterns.

The instructions in this book explain how to make findings using hand tools, but many of the same findings can also be made using a jig. Deciding whether to use this tool is a personal choice that depends on many factors, but primarily it is a subjective judgment made by each individual jewelry designer. Either way, it is important to make an informed decision. Jig users range from jewelry artists who must make jewelry in volume to beginners who are not comfortable primarily using hand tools. Depending on your skill level, intent, and taste, a wire jig can be a valuable tool in your collection.

For beginners, jigs are convenient and most jig manufacturers provide free instructions and patterns with the purchase of a jig. Wigjig.com goes even further than this and provides an extensive online library of free projects and information on its website. This company also sells books and other related supplies and equipment so beginners can find everything they need to get started using a jig.

Another type of jewelry maker who sometimes prefers to use a jig instead of hand tools is the production artist. Perhaps you are running a small jewelry business and you need a way to make duplicate pieces in fairly large quantities. Jigs are an option you may want to consider because they provide a way to make more than one piece at a time. As you wrap your wire around the pegs, you can begin to stack one design on top of another. You then remove and cut apart the wire components.

Finally, the third type of jeweler who tends to use a jig is one who prefers the look of precision pieces. As with any new tool or technique, learning to use a jig properly takes time. However, once you learn, it offers a way to make wire pieces that all look the same, almost machine-made. A jig isn't really a machine, but it does eliminate some of the guesswork that goes along with using hand tools.

Ultimately, you need to decide whether a jig is right for you. If you are new to wire work, a jig can provide a level of comfort, and more experienced wire artists who prefer a more uniform appearance or need to make large quantities of jewelry should also consider this tool.

Types of Jigs

Differences in jig designs range from materials used to the sizes offered. Some manufacturers use lightweight plastic, and though these may be more economical than most, they can easily break, as can the plastic pegs and accessories that accompany them. On the other end of the spectrum is metal, which can be used to make both the peg board and the pegs that you insert into the board. Finally, another variety, made by www.wigjig.com, is a combination of metal and plastic. The board part of the jig is made of a clear, high-quality plastic that is transparent but thicker than the economy jigs, and the pegs are metal.

Along with jig materials, the size of a jig can vary greatly. Larger jigs with large-diameter holes in the board are made for larger components and thicker wire than smaller similar jig designs. Models of jigs can vary greatly between different suppliers, so for more specifics, it's best to check directly with the jig manufacturer for model variations and the specifications that apply to each one.

Jig Patterns

Although jig manufacturers often provide plenty of information as far as creating components, once you become proficient with a jig, you'll be able to come up with your own wire designs. The next step is to create a jig pattern for your designs. To figure out the pattern, which refers to the arrangement of your pegs on your board, remember that each loop or curl on your component needs to have a peg stationed on your board. The space between the pegs will equal the amount of wire between your loops. One option for creating your own jig patterns is to use graph paper, and each box on the paper equals one hole in your board. For example, to make a **Triple Loop Eye Pin**, you will need three pegs, one for each loop. Then you will need to position these on the board in a triangular pattern.

Jig Tips

Here are a few tips and ideas to help you when working with wire jigs:

- Be patient. While learning any new method, don't expect instant success. Give yourself time to practice with economy wire before you start expecting "perfect" results.

- Read the instructions. Most jig manufacturers offer written instructions. Take advantage of them.

- Determine your purpose, then select the jig that is right for you. If you make delicate pieces, don't try to make them on a jig that has large pegs and is designed for making larger components.

- Consider wire gauge. The size of the wire, or gauge, that you prefer to work with will affect the pieces you make, so think about this when you select a jig.

- Use appropriate pegs for a project. The pegs used on a jig come in different diameters. Remember that these replace your round-nosed pliers; therefore, the diameter of the peg will determine the size of your loop. It seems pretty basic—large pegs make large loops and small pegs make small loops—but this is an important consideration when you are setting up your jig.

- Experiment with shapes. Pegs are primarily round, but you can get them in different shapes, such as squares and triangles. A variety of peg shapes will give you a variety of design options.

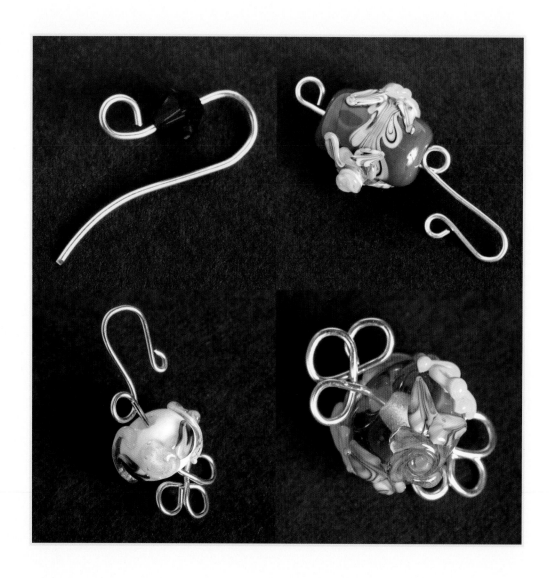

JEWELRY TECHNIQUES

Findings, when compared with beads and jewelry components, are often considered the less glamorous part of making jewelry. Ask the average jewelry maker and she will often admit to having enough beads to fill an auditorium but only enough findings to fill a coffee cup. However, finished pieces of jewelry could not exist without ear hooks, headpins, and clasps. Unique findings can also add a wonderful design element to your jewelry pieces. With a little wire and a few hand tools, you can easily make some of your own findings to accent your jewelry.

EARRING FINDINGS

Basic beaded earrings are normally made up of an ear hook and a headpin. These components are generally referred to as "findings," and they help form the structure of a jewelry piece. An ear hook allows the wearer to insert the earring through a pierced ear while the head-pin is used to attach beads or other pieces to the ear hook, thus creating a dangle effect. Most jewelry making suppliers who sell beads and wire will also sell manufactured findings, and the variety available for purchase is tremendous. However, making earring findings, such as ear hooks and headpins, is not that difficult, and it's a helpful skill to learn for a few reasons. First, it's very convenient. Sometimes it just isn't possible to have all the supplies on hand that you need. Rather than running to a local bead store or putting in another jewelry supply order, you can quickly create the findings you need to complete your jewelry design right away. Another advantage is that it's very economical to be able to make your own earring findings using sterling or gold-filled wire. The cost of precious metal wire is very reasonable, especially when bought in bulk. Literally, wire can cost just pennies per inch. Finally, having the ability to make findings adds a lot to the overall craftsmanship of a piece; the artist can proudly state that she made the components herself. For the earring projects in this book (unless otherwise specified), I use 21-gauge (.71 mm), half-hard, round sterling wire. 21-gauge, both half-hard and soft, is my favorite gauge to use because it is so versatile. I have found that it is thin enough to go through a pierced hole in your ear and also fits through most beads, but at the same time it is strong enough to handle the weight of the finished earring. Thinner 22-gauge (.65 mm) also works well for most earring findings, and I have even heard of artists using 20-gauge (.80 mm). The earring findings described in this section combine similar techniques to create a variety of designs, so you will use many of the same tools (as listed in the Basic Tool Kit section, page 31) to create each piece.

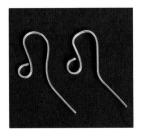

Project 1: Basic Ear Hooks

This style of earring hook is often referred to as French wires or fishhooks. Whatever you call them, you only need a few hand tools and a few inches of wire to make a pair.

Materials

- 3 ½" (9 cm) piece of wire
- basic tool kit (see page 31)

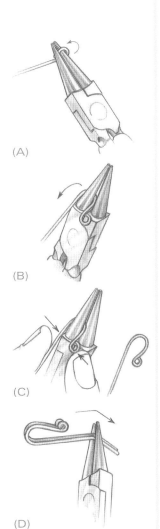

(A)

(B)

(C)

(D)

1. Begin by cutting the wire in half so that you have two pieces that are 1 ¾" (4.5 cm) each, and then use a jewelers' file to smooth the ends of each piece.

2. With round-nosed-pliers, create a small loop on one end of one piece of wire (A).

3. Repeat this for the other piece of wire, ensuring that the second loop is the same size as the first.

4. Next, hold both pieces of wire together so the loops are lined up next to each other.

5. With the thickest part of your round-nosed pliers, grasp the straight part of your wires approximately ¼" (.6 cm) past the loops, and use your fingers to bend both wires 180 degrees around the nose. You want to bend both wires at the same time so they match (B).

6. The next step is a very small, subtle movement, but it will help make the hook a little more rounded. Using the round-nosed pliers, position the largest part of the nose inside the bent area, approximately ¼" (.6 cm) from the curl. The pliers' nose should point up and the wire curl should be positioned horizontally toward you. Gently squeeze the curl and the flat part of the ear hook towards each other about 5 degrees (C).

7. Hold both ear hooks side by side again. This time, use the middle area on the nose of the pliers, and measuring about ¼" (.6 cm) away from the ends, slightly bend the ends of both wires (approximately 25 degrees) at the same time (D).

Jeweler's Tip:

If you are a little nervous about making your first pair of ear hooks, purchase a pair and use them as a guide or template while you work. It will help you visualize the finished product.

Project 2: Beaded Ear Hooks

Once you have mastered making **Basic Ear Hooks**, you can easily jazz it up by adding a bead and using a little more wire. These hooks are also a great way to connect the look of your finding with your earring design.

Materials

- 4" (10 cm) piece of wire
- two 4-mm or 6-mm beads of your choice
- basic tool kit (see page 31)

1. Begin by cutting the wire in half so that you have two pieces that are 2" (5 cm) each, and then use a jewelers' file to smooth the ends of each piece.

2. As described in steps 2 and 3 of the **Basic Ear Hooks**, make a small loop on each piece of wire.

(A)

3. Now slip one bead onto each piece of wire, and push the bead up against the loops you just made (A).

4. As described in step 5 of the **Basic Ear Hooks**, take one of the wire and bead pieces and wrap the wire around the round-nosed pliers, but this time position the pliers ¼" (.6 cm) from the bead that is resting next to the loop (B).

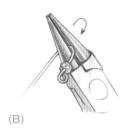

(B)

5. Repeat the previous step for your second ear hook.

6. Again, refer to the instructions above for the **Basic Ear Hooks**, and follow steps 6 and 7 for each ear hook to make complete pair.

Jeweler's Tip:

Because of the addition of the beads to the ear hooks, it is too awkward to hold and bend them at the same time. However, to help make sure they match as closely as possible when you're finished, it's a good idea to repeat each step of the instructions for each piece rather than making one ear hook from beginning to end and then making a second one to match.

Project 3: Triple Loop Ear Hooks

Here is another adaptation of the **Basic Ear Hooks** project. You'll notice that many of the same steps are used, so once you've mastered the first type of hook, you'll be ready to tackle this design.

Materials

- 6" (15 cm) piece of wire
- basic tool kit (see page 31)

(A)

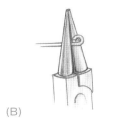

(B)

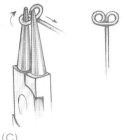

(C)

(D)

1. Cut the wire in half so that you have two pieces that are 3" (7.5 cm) each, and then use a jewelers' file to smooth the ends of each piece.

2. Using the end of the round-nosed pliers, make a small loop on the end of one piece of wire (A).

3. Hold the wire with the round-nosed pliers and position the end of the pliers' nose against the first loop (B).

4. Make a second loop by using your fingers to grasp the straight part of the wire, and wrapping it 360 degrees around the nose of the pliers (C).

5. Make a third loop next to the second loop the same way you did in the two previous steps (D).

(Continued on page 44)

(E)

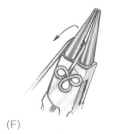

(F)

(G)

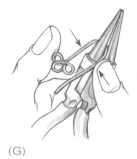

(H)

6. Gently flatten the loops using nylon-nosed pliers (E).

7. The rest of the steps are very similar to those for the **Basic Ear Hook**, but now you work on one ear hook at a time. Grasp the straight part of the wire approximately ¼" (.6 cm) past the loops with the thickest part of your round-nosed pliers, and use your fingers to wrap the wire 180 degrees around the nose (F).

8. For a more rounded affect, position the largest part of the round-nosed pliers inside the area you just bent, and gently squeeze the loop part and flat part of the ear hook toward each other about 5 degrees (G).

9. Use the middle area on the nose of the pliers, and measuring about ¼" (.63 cm) away from the end of your hook, slightly bend the end of the wire (approximately 25 degrees) (H).

10. Repeat the previous steps for the second ear hook.

Jeweler's Tip:

Always use a jewelers' file to ensure that the ends of the wire are smooth to the touch. It only takes a few minutes and is well worth the time to make sure that your finished piece is comfortable for the wearer.

Project 4: Curly Headpin

Once you make your own ear hooks, you will want to make your own headpins, too. This headpin design is very easy, and it looks really nice on a finished pair of earrings.

Materials

- 5" (12.5 cm) piece of wire
- basic tool kit (see page 31)

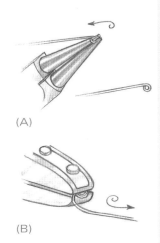

(A)

(B)

1. Cut the wire in half so that you have two pieces that are 2 ½" (6 cm) each, and then use a jewelers' file to smooth the ends of each piece.

2. Using round-nosed pliers, make a small curl at the end of one piece of wire (A).

3. To continue curling, hold the small curl with nylon-nosed pliers, and use your fingers to bend the straight part of the wire toward and around the first curl you made in the previous step (B).

4. Make the curl as small or large as you like. However, remember to leave enough room to allow for beads and a loop at the top when connecting it to the earring wire.

5. Repeat steps 2 through 4 to make the second headpin.

Jeweler's Tip:

"Practice makes perfect" is an old saying, but it still rings true, especially when working with wire. You aren't a machine, so don't expect each loop, curl, and bend of the wire to be perfect. In fact, that's part of the beauty of handcrafted artwork. However, you'll find the more you twist and curl, the better you'll become at making your findings consistent.

Project 5: Double Loop Eye Pin

This double loop eye pin uses the same method as the **Triple Loop Ear Hook** project. However, these are much easier to make because, basically, they consist of two small loops on the end of a piece of wire—simple yet effective.

Materials

- 6" (15 cm) piece of wire
- basic tool kit (see page 31)

(A)

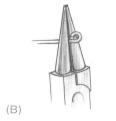

(B)

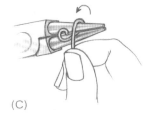

(C)

(D)

1. Cut the piece of wire in half, and file the ends smooth.

2. Using the end of the round-nosed pliers, make a small loop on the end of one piece of wire (A).

3. Hold the wire with the round-nosed pliers and position the end of the nose against the first loop (B).

4. Make a second loop by using your fingers, holding the straight part of the wire and wrapping it 180 degrees around the nose of the pliers (C).

5. Gently flatten the loops using nylon-nosed pliers, and at the same time, use your fingers to bend the straight wire so that it is positioned vertically over the loops (D).

6. Repeat steps 2 through 5 to complete a pair.

Jeweler's Tip:

Flattening the loops with nylon-nosed pliers gives these a more finished look and will help keep the loops from catching on anything. This is one example that illustrates how useful these unusual pliers can be when you are working with wire.

Project 6: Triple Loop Eye Pin

You have probably guessed already that this is yet another adaptation of the **Triple Loop Ear Hook**. You'll find this eye pin much easier to make than its sister ear hook. As with any eye pin or headpin, the length of the finished piece can vary depending on how long you want your earrings. The longer the earrings, the more wire you'll need, but for an average length, the instructions below are a good way to get started.

Materials

- 6" (15 cm) piece of wire
- basic tool kit (see page 31)

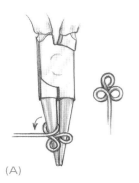

(A)

1. Follow steps 1 through 6 of the **Triple Loop Ear Hook** instructions on page 43 (A).

Jeweler's Tip:

Remember that this technique can be used with a variety of wire gauges. Before deciding on which gauge you need, you'll want to make sure the wire fits through the beads you plan to use. Although 21-gauge (.71 mm) wire fits through most beads, it does not normally fit through pearls. Often a smaller gauge, such as 24-gauge (.5 mm), will be necessary.

JUMP RINGS, HOOKS, AND CLASPS

How a jewelry piece is attached to the wearer is crucial. Clasps, hooks, and jump rings are important elements to any jewelry design because, without them, we could all lose some beautiful jewelry. Although 21-gauge (.71 mm) is an excellent gauge for just about any design, when making clasps, it's a good idea to use a fairly strong gauge of wire. If possible, try to stick to at least 20-gauge (.8 mm) for any finding that works as a clasp in your finished jewelry design. Unless otherwise specified, 20-gauge (.8 mm) is used for all the findings in this section. These findings should be attractive and strong at the same time, and though they are practical, necessary pieces to our jewelry, we do not have to hide them from view. Instead, we can integrate them into our designs.

Project 1: Basic Jump Ring

Jump rings are just simple wire circles, but they have a multitude of uses when it comes to making jewelry. The size of the jump rings you make depends on the diameter of the dowel, and the number of jump rings you make will depend on the amount of wire you use.

Materials

- 6" (15 cm) piece of wire
- wooden dowel, pencil, or pen
- basic tool kit (see page 31)

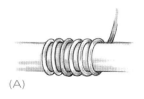

(A)

(B)

(C)

(D)

1. Begin by using your fingers to wrap the wire around the dowel so that the wire is flush against it (A).

2. Slide the wire off the dowel so that you have a coil of wire.

3. Use a pair of flush-cut wire cutters to cut each coil one time to create a single ring (B).

4. Finally, use a jeweler's file to smooth the ends of the wire you just cut so that both ends of the jump ring are flat and can fit flush together (C and D).

Jeweler's Tip:

Try working with at least a 6" (15 cm) piece of wire when you make components or findings. Although you may need only an inch or two to make a hook or clasp, sometimes it can be much easier to work with a longer piece of wire, and you'll still have enough wire to make something else with the leftovers.

Project 2: Basic Hook

This is one instance in which it might be easier to work with a 6" (15 cm) piece of wire, though you don't need that much to complete this findings project successfully. It's really a matter of preference. Some jewelry makers find it easier to work with a longer piece of wire and some don't, but it's worth trying.

Materials

- 1 ½" (3.5 cm) piece of wire
- basic tool kit (see page 31)

(A)

1. After filing the ends of the wire, take the round-nosed pliers and make a loop or curl on one end of the wire (A).

2. Now, measuring approximately ½" (1.25 cm) from the end of the curl, grasp the wire with the round-nosed pliers using the middle part of the pliers' nose.

3. Holding the pliers with one hand, use your other hand to wrap the wire around the nose of the pliers to create a "hook" shape (B).

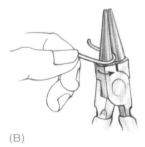

(B)

4. Using the round-nosed pliers, create a tiny curl on the end of the hook you created in the previous step (C).

(C)

Jeweler's Tip:

Store your unused wire in an airtight container such as a large zip-lock bag or plastic bowl with a lid. As sterling is exposed to oxygen, it oxidizes and tarnish will build up on your wire. Label the outside of the bag or bowl with the wire gauge to help avoid confusion.

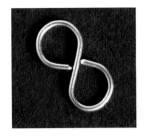

Project 3: Basic Eye

By using a little wire, you can fashion this **Basic Eye** design, which takes the form of a figure-eight. The two loops on this piece combine to work as the second part of a clasp, which is made to team up with any number of hook-style clasps.

Materials

- 1 ½" (3.75 cm) piece of wire
- basic tool kit (see page 31)

(A)

(B)

1. Start by using a jeweler's file to smooth both ends of the wire.

2. Now use the round-nosed pliers to make a large loop on one end of the wire so that you have used up half of the piece of wire (A).

3. Do the same on the other end of the wire, but this time the loop should be facing in the other direction so that you make a figure-eight (8) with the wire (B).

Jeweler's Tip:

Keep your wire scraps in separate plastic bags, one for each type of metal (sterling silver, fine silver, gold-filled, and copper). You never know when you need just a little piece of wire. Plus, some wire vendors will give you credit for your metal scraps.

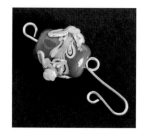

Project 4: Beaded Hook

Once you learn how to make the **Basic Hook**, this variation will seem so obvious. Of course, remember that the amount of wire you will need may vary depending on the size of the bead you add to your hook: The smaller the bead, the less wire you will need; the larger the bead, the more wire you will need. However, the instructions below are a good place to start.

Materials:

- 3" (7.5 cm) piece of wire
- choice of bead
- basic tool kit (see page 31)

(A)

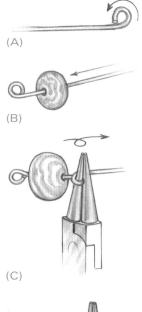

(B)

(C)

(D)

(E)

1. After filing the ends of the wire, use round-nosed pliers to make a small loop or curl on one end of the wire (A).

2. Add your choice of bead onto the wire (lampwork beads are excellent for these enhanced hooks) (B).

3. Now position the narrowest part of the round-nosed pliers' nose about ¼" (.6 cm) past your bead, and grasp the wire with the nose.

4. While holding the pliers in one hand, use your other hand to wrap the wire completely around (360 degrees) the nose of the pliers (C).

5. Measuring approximately ½" (1 cm) from the end of the loop created in the previous step, grasp the wire with the round-nosed pliers using the middle part of the pliers' nose.

6. Holding the pliers with one hand, use your other hand to wrap the wire around the nose of the pliers to create a "hook" shape (D).

7. Using the round-nosed pliers, create a tiny curl on the end of the hook you created in the previous step (E).

Jeweler's Tip:

Always use less expensive "practice wire," such as copper or galvanized wire, when you are learning a new technique because it's safe to assume that you won't make a perfect piece on your first try. Although it may not be as soft and easy to use as sterling or gold-filled, you won't waste as much of your good wire this way.

Project 5: Triple Loop Hook

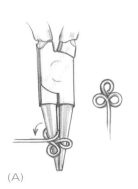

This design combines the **Basic Hook** method with the **Triple Loop Eye Pin** method. When you look at the finished finding, you can literally see where one design ends and another begins. Use the center loop of the finished hook to attach a single strand of beads, or if you want to create a triple strand of beads for a necklace or bracelet, you can use all three loops on this hook.

Materials

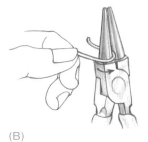

- 3" (7.5 cm) piece of wire
- basic tool kit (see page 31)

1. Follow steps 1 through 3 of the **Triple Loop Eye Pin** instructions on page 47 (A).

2. Now, follow steps 2 through 4 of the **Basic Hook** instructions on page 50 (B and C).

(A)

(B)

(C)

Jeweler's Tip:

There is never just one way to do anything, and this is especially true when it comes to working with wire. You may learn one technique from the instructions in this book, find another slightly different method described on the Internet, and then turn around and figure out by yourself a third way for accomplishing the same task. That's one of the great things about making jewelry. The possibilities are endless, so be open to them.

Project 6: Triple Loop Beaded Hook

This hook design continues the loop trend used so far, and it combines the same basic principles of the **Beaded Hook** and the **Triple Loop Hook**. Again, any time you add a bead to a hook design, you need to take into consideration the size of the bead when determining how much wire you need.

Materials

- 4" (10 cm) piece of wire
- basic tool kit (see page 31)

1. Follow steps 1 through 3 of the **Triple Loop Eye Pin** instructions on page 47 (A).

2. Now, follow steps 2 through 7 of the **Beaded Hook** instructions on page 52 (B and C).

Jeweler's Tip:

The wire lengths listed for all projects in this book are a gauge and can vary depending on your beads and the size of the loops you make. It's always better to have too much than not enough wire. If your wire is too short, it can become very awkward to work with.

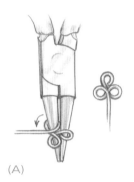

(A)

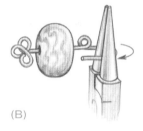

(B)

(C)

Project 7: Double Strand Clasp

Double the beauty of your jewelry designs by creating double strand jewelry pieces. It's easy once you learn how to make this **Double Strand Clasp**. This clasp has two pieces: One is the hook; the other is the eye. Loops and wraps continue to help you in this findings technique.

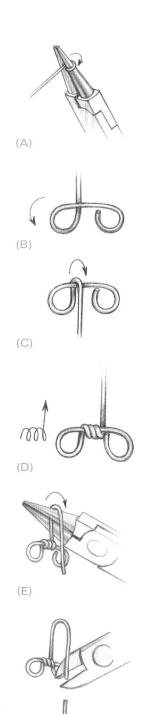

(A)

(B)

(C)

(D)

(E)

(F)

Materials

- 10" (25 cm) piece of wire
- basic tool kit (see page 31)

1. Beginning with the hook side of the clasp, file both ends of the wire, and then use round-nosed pliers to curl one end of the wire so you have one loop (A).

2. Make another loop approximately ½" (1 cm) away from the first loop so there is a small space between them (B).

3. Now wrap the remaining wire around the space between the two loops. You should have enough space to wrap the wire two or three times and end with the wire positioned straight up and pointing in the opposite direction of the two loops (C and D).

4. Position the round-nosed pliers about 1" (2.5 cm) from the bottom of the wire, and use your fingers or flat-nosed pliers to bend the wire around the pliers' nose (E).

5. Measure a little more than 1" (2.5 cm) past the bend you just made, and use wire cutters to trim off excess wire (F).

(Continued on page 56)

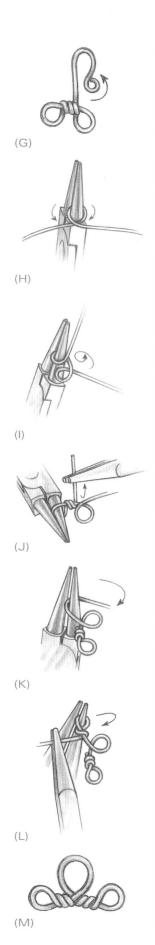

(G)

(H)

(I)

(J)

(K)

(L)

(M)

6. File the end of the wire, and then use round-nosed pliers to add a tiny curl to the end of the wire (G).

7. For the eye segment of the clasp, file both ends of the leftover wire.

8. Locate the center of the wire piece. Hold this with the largest area of the round-nosed pliers' nose, and bend both ends of the wire in opposite directions around the nose to make a loop in the middle of the wire (H).

9. Add a slightly smaller loop next to the loop you just made (I).

10. Continue to hold the nose of the pliers in the smaller loop and use flat-nosed pliers to wrap the excess wire around itself (J). (This is the same technique used for the **Wrapped Loop** on page 60.)

11. Repeat steps 9 and 10 for the other side of the eye segment (K, L, and M).

Jeweler's Tip:

By changing the type of wire you use, you can add more complexity to your findings. Of course, it will only look more complex. The methods will change very little, so once you have mastered a technique, consider using square or even twisted wire next time.

Project 8: Quadruple Loop Eye

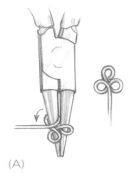

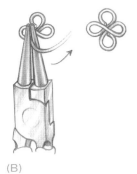

(A)

(B)

One of the most versatile findings in this book, the **Quadruple Loop Eye** can serve double duty as a partner for a hook or as a decorative internal element in your design. It's amazing what you can do with a little wire and a few loops.

Materials

- 4" (10 cm) piece of wire
- basic tool kit (see page 31)

1. Follow steps 1 through 3 of the **Triple Loop Eye Pin** on page 47 (A).

2. Place the round-nosed pliers' nose next to the third loop, and make a fourth loop right next to it (B).

3. Trim off the excess wire and file the end smooth.

4. Flatten the loops on your eye component by gently compressing it with nylon-nosed pliers.

Jeweler's Tip:

When making findings using hand tools versus a jig, consistency can be a challenge. To help ensure your loops are relatively the same size, position your wire at the same spot on the nose of your pliers. To help you remember, try marking the spot on the nose with a permanent marker or a piece of masking tape.

Project 9: Beaded Loop Eye

Combine the **Triple Loop Eye** finding with your favorite bead. Lampwork beads work great for this because many of them have fairly large holes. You won't want to hide this part of your clasp behind the back of your neck.

Materials

- 6" (15 cm) piece of wire
- choice of bead
- basic tool kit (see page 31)

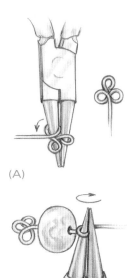

(A)

(B)

1. Follow steps 1 through 3 of the **Triple Loop Eye Pin** instructions on page 47 (A).
2. Slide your choice of bead onto the wire.
3. Make three more loops on the other side of the bead (B).
4. Trim off the extra wire and file the end of the wire.
5. Use nylon-nosed pliers to compress the last three loops.

Jeweler's Tip:

If you want to use beads on your finding but have problems because the hole of the bead is too small for the wire, consider using a smaller gauge. Often, you can go down a gauge size without causing major structural problems for the jewelry piece you are making.

BEAD AND WIRE TECHNIQUES

Once you learn to make your own findings, you also need to understand how to connect all the elements of your jewelry designs. This is when a number of different jewelry-making methods are required. Below are instructions for some of the most often used techniques for creating bead and wire jewelry.

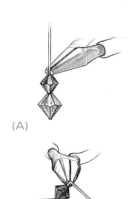
(A)

(B)

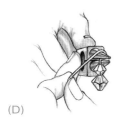
(C)

(D)

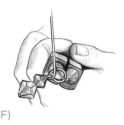
(E)

(F)

(G)

Wrapped Loop

The wrapped loop technique is extremely useful for a large number of jewelry projects. You can use it to make earrings, add dangles to necklaces, or finish off a clasp for a bracelet. For this technique, you will need a pair of round-nosed pliers, wire cutters, flat-nosed pliers, a jeweler's file, and your choice of wire to create wrapped loops.

1. Start by using either flat- or round-nosed pliers to bend the wire at a 90-degree angle so that you create an upside-down L shape (A and B).

2. Position the nose of the round-nosed pliers in the bend that you created in the previous step (C).

3. Use your fingers to wrap the wire around the nose of the pliers to form a loop (D).

4. While keeping the round-nosed pliers inside the loop, hold the loop against the nose of the pliers with one finger (E). You should have the round-nosed pliers in one hand with one finger pressing the loop against the nose. (If you are right handed, then you will probably want to use your left hand to hold the pliers and your pointer finger to hold the loop against the nose.)

5. Using your other hand (if you are right handed, the right hand), start to wrap the loose wire around the straight piece of wire that is directly under your loop. If the wire is soft, you can probably do this with your fingers. Otherwise, use bent-nosed (or flat-nosed, if you prefer) pliers to hold the loose wire and wrap (F).

6. Continue to wrap as many times as you want; if necessary, trim off excess wire with wire cutters and file the ends smooth with a jeweler's file (G).

7. Use the bent-nosed pliers to press the wire-wrapped end flat to make sure it does not scratch or poke the wearer.

8. If necessary, use the round-nosed pliers to straighten the loop.

Jeweler's Tip:

Do you have lots of curious hands or playful paws helping you making jewelry? If you have young children or animals, beads can be a magnet for them, so keep small items in a safe place. Tackle boxes and utility boxes available at your local hardware store will help you stay organized while your family stays safe.

Simple Loop

This technique is a simplified version of the wrapped loop technique and is useful for making earrings, dangles, pendants, and various other jewelry components. Although wrapping is more secure, if done properly, this simple loop technique can also be surprisingly strong. For this procedure, you will need a pair of round-nosed pliers, wire cutters, and a headpin. A headpin is being used for illustration purposes; however, you can also use this technique with wire.

(A)

1. Use the round-nosed pliers to bend the headpin at a 90-degree angle (A).

2. Make sure the part of the headpin that is bent is about ½" (1 cm) long; if necessary, trim any excess with wire cutters.

3. Position the bent part of the headpin so that it is facing away from you.

(B)

4. Then, using round-nosed pliers, grasp the end of the bent headpin and make sure the middle part of the pliers' nose is holding the pin. After positioning the pliers correctly, curl the wire slowly toward you (B).

5. Because the first curl will probably not complete the entire loop, release and reposition your pliers on the loop you have started.

6. Continue to curl it toward you until you have made a full circle (C).

(C)

Jeweler's Tip:

When working with multiple pliers and tools, it's sometimes helpful to place a soft towel over your work area. This allows you to pick up and set down your tools quickly without making a lot of "thunking" noises.

Crimp Beads

A beaded piece of jewelry can be finished on the ends a number of different ways, and using crimp beads to do this is one popular method. Some jewelry makers prefer the look of crimp beads to bead tips, but it is really a matter of personal preference. To use this method, you'll need a pair of crimping pliers, crimp beads (I highly recommend using tube-shaped crimp beads versus round crimp beads because they are much easier to work with), round-nosed pliers, wire cutters, and beading wire. As with bead tips, you need to understand how to start and finish with crimp beads because there are a few minor differences.

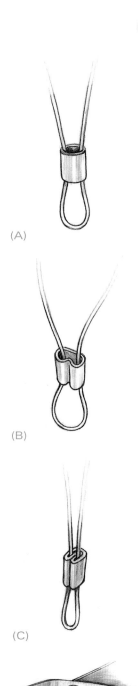

(A)

(B)

(C)

(D)

1. Slide one crimp bead onto the end of a piece of beading wire, and loop the wire back through the crimp bead (A).

2. Position the crimp bead inside the second notch in the crimping pliers (the one closest to you when you are holding the pliers in your hand), and close the pliers around the bead. You should see that the crimp bead now has a groove down the middle so that it curls (B).

3. Now, position the same crimp bead in the first notch in the pliers, and close the pliers around it so that you flatten the curl (C and D).

4. Use wire cutters to trim off all but about ¼" (.6 cm) of excess beading wire.

5. Add your beads, making sure you slide the first bead over both pieces of wire on the end.

6. Once you have strung all your beads, you are ready to finish the other end. Slide a second crimp bead onto the end of your wire after the last bead strung.

7. Loop the wire back through the crimp bead as well as the last bead of the piece.

8. Insert the nose of the round-nosed pliers into the loop.

9. While holding the round-nosed pliers with one hand, gently pull the beading wire with your other hand so that you push the crimp bead up against the other beads. This will ensure that you do not have any extra slack in your beaded piece and that you also keep the end loop of your beading wire intact.

10. Repeat steps 2 and 3 above to close the crimp bead.

11. Finish by using wire cutters to trim off excess beading wire carefully.

Jeweler's Tip:

Keep your tools in an extra large coffee cup so you can carry them around and work in different areas of your house. Just hang one side of your pliers inside the cup and the other outside. You'll be surprised how many pliers fit.

Bead Tips

Bead tips are small, metal findings used to start and finish off a beaded piece, such as a bracelet or necklace. Some people refer to them as clamshells because they have two cups that are open and look just like a clam. Attached to the cup is a small hook that attaches to a clasp or a jump ring. You will need to attach bead tips to the beginning and end of a piece. In addition to bead tips, you will need your choice of cord (such as nylon or beading wire), flat-nosed pliers, scissors, jewelers' glue, and an awl or corsage pin.

1. To connect a bead tip to the beginning of a piece of beaded jewelry, start by tying at least two overhand knots, one on top of the other, at the end of your cord.

2. Slide the unknotted end of your cord down through the hole in the middle of the bead tip, and pull the cord so that the knot rests inside one of the shells (A).

3. Trim off the excess cord with scissors or wire cutters, and drop a small amount of jeweler's glue onto your knots.

(A)

(Continued on page 64)

(B)

(C)

4. Use flat-nosed pliers to close the two shells of the bead tip together (B and C).

5. String all of your beads.

6. When you are ready to finish the piece, add another bead tip to the end by slipping the cord through the hole in the bead tip so that the open part of the bead tip (the shells) is facing away from the beads previously strung.

7. Tie a loose overhand knot with your cord, and insert an awl (or a corsage pin) into the knot.

8. Hold the cord with one hand and the awl with your other hand.

9. Use the awl to push the knot down into the bead tip, and pull tightly on the cord with your other hand.

10. Slip the awl out of the knot, and make another knot using this method, making sure that both knots fit inside one of the shells.

11. Trim off the excess cord, and drop a small amount of glue onto your knots.

12. Finish by using flat-nosed pliers to close the two shells of the bead tip together.

Jeweler's Tip:

Once you start working with wire frequently, you'll discover that little files show up all over the house, and some just disappear into thin air. So that you always have a file handy, it's a good idea to own more than one file set. They are fairly affordable, so the cost is worth it.

Knotting

Knotting between beads is a technique used by many jewelry makers when stringing high-end beads such as pearls. The knots between the beads allow for a nice draping effect when finished, and they also have a practical purpose. If a knotted necklace were to break, the beads would not roll off the strand. Also, the knots create a little space between the beads so they do not rub against each other. This is especially important for pearls or other soft beads. To knot between your beads, you need a beading awl (a corsage pin also works well); silk or nylon cord with an attached, twisted-wire needle; and your choice of beads.

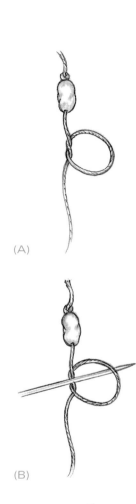

(A)

1. Start by finishing one end of your cord in the technique you prefer. I normally use the **Bead Tips** technique (page 63) for this.

2. Once your necklace is started, string your first bead onto the wire needle on the cord and push it down to the end of your necklace.

3. Tie a loose overhand knot (A).

4. Insert the beading awl through the loose knot (B).

5. Next, use one hand to push the awl and knot down toward the bead and hold onto the cord with your other hand until the awl and knot are flush up against the bead (C).

6. Keeping the knot up against the bead, carefully slip the end of the awl out of the knot and immediately use your fingers to push the knot against the bead.

7. Repeat this method for each bead that you wish to knot between.

(B)

Jeweler's Tip:

If you don't have an awl or a corsage pin handy and need to tie knots, try using a stickpin. They also work really well because they are heavy enough to handle pressure but thin enough to fit inside a bead tip.

(C)

BEAD AND WIRE PROJECTS

Now it's time to create beautiful jewelry using your own handcrafted wire findings. This section provides step-by-step instructions for jewelry designs that
incorporate the methods described in the techniques section of this book.
Either follow them to the letter or use them as inspirational jumping-off points
for your own signature jewelry creations.

GLITTER AND GOLD EARRINGS

Gold-filled wire, gold-colored pearls, and sparkling two-tone crystal beads combine to create an eye-catching pair of earrings that will spend very little time hidden away in a jewelry box. The addition of the **Triple Loop Eye Pins** and **Basic Ear Hooks**, which you can craft yourself, provide an elegant accent to the finished pair. Although these earrings are obviously hand-crafted, they can also be worn with any of your fine gold jewelry, such as gold chains, omega necklaces, or even tennis-style bracelets. Once you make these, you'll find yourself picking them up again and again on those busy mornings when you grab your favorite gold jewelry before rushing out the door.

Materials

- 6" (15 cm) of 24-gauge (.5 mm) gold-filled wire
- 3 ½" (9 cm) of 21-gauge (.71 mm) gold-filled wire
- two 4-mm dark purple crystal beads
- two 6-mm light amethyst-colored crystal beads
- two 8-mm gold-colored pearl beads
- basic tool kit (see page 31)

1. First, using the 21-gauge (.71 mm) gold-filled wire, make one pair of **Basic Ear Hooks**.

2. Then, using the 24-gauge (.5 mm) gold-filled wire, make one pair of **Triple Loop Eye Pins**.

3. Take one of the eye pins and slide on beads in the following order: one light amethyst-colored crystal, one pearl, and one dark purple crystal.

4. Next, using round- and flat-nosed pliers, create a **Wrapped Loop** on the end of the eye pin.

5. You are now ready to attach your **Basic Ear Hook**. Using flat-nosed pliers, gently open the loop on the ear hook, slip on the **Wrapped Loop**, and again use flat-nosed pliers to close the ear hook loop.

6. Repeat steps 3 through 5 above to make another earring so that you have a matching pair.

Jeweler's Tip:

Pearl beads have very small holes, so make sure the wire you select fits through the hole in your pearls before you start any wire and pearl project. Although the size of the holes will vary, the thickest wire you might be able to use is 21-gauge (.71 mm). Most often, you will need to use 24- to 26-gauge (.5 to .4 mm).

Design Advice:

Feel free to break the rules on occasion. Classic looks never go out of style, but if you want a one-of-kind design that will get noticed, try to think outside your jewelry box now and then. Odd color and textural combinations, an eclectic combination of beads and components, or an asymmetrical assembly of items can sometimes send you on your way to creating some of your most interesting designs.

Variation Idea:

Assemble a matching necklace in just a few minutes by repeating this earring design and adding a few more materials to your list. The techniques are the same: **Triple Loop Eye Pins** and **Wrapped Loop**. Just add a gold-colored center component and some pretty organza ribbon, and you'll be able to make a matching earring and necklace set to wear the same day. To keep your ribbon from fraying, make sure to cut your ribbon at an angle and apply a tiny amount of clear glue on the end.

JACKIE O NECKLACE

Pearls instantly denote classic fashion. A simple strand of pearls became an icon when the rich and famous, the likes of Jacqueline Kennedy Onassis and Princess Grace, unconsciously defined the notion of class and sophistication through their fashion choices. This double strand of silver-colored pearls, amethyst gemstones, and jet crystals on a sterling silver **Double Strand Clasp** is reminiscent of an era of elegance. The simple, symmetrical design combines two matching strands of beads on a sterling clasp that you can make yourself. Twist the strands together or wear them loose so they fall against each other.

Materials

- 10" (25 cm) of 20-gauge (.8 mm) round sterling wire
- thirty-seven 6-mm gray-colored freshwater pearls
- seventy-four 4-mm jet AB crystal beads
- thirty-five 4-mm amethyst beads
- four sterling bead tips
- 4' (1.2 m) of medium-weight beading wire
- basic tool kit (see page 31)

1. Using 20-gauge (.8 mm) sterling wire, make a **Double Strand Clasp,** and set this aside to attach after you string your beads.

2. Cut a few feet of beading wire, and then attach a bead tip to one end of the wire.

3. For the outside necklace strand, slip on one jet bead, one pearl, one jet bead, and one amethyst bead. Repeat this pattern 18 times.

4. Complete the strand with one jet bead, one pearl, and one jet bead.

5. Then finish this strand of beads with another bead tip.

6. For the inside strand, repeat steps 2 through 5 above, but this time repeat the pattern only 17 times.

7. Use round-nosed pliers to curl the bead tip hooks around the loops on each end of your **Double Strand Clasp**.

Jeweler's Tip:

A multistrand bead board is helpful when working on a piece that has more than one strand of beads. Each groove in the board is marked at ½" (1 cm) and 1" (2.5 cm) increments to make it easier to accurately determine the length of each strand, whether you want to make each about the same length (as in the Jackie O Necklace) or prefer your strands to be in graduated lengths.

Design Advice:

It can be fun to look through fashion magazines for inspiration, and though it is important for designers to be conscious of the latest fashions, it is equally important to be careful about becoming a slave to fashion. If you want to make unique jewelry, then you don't want to copy the latest fashion fads. You want to start your own!

Variation Idea:

Pearls are also included in this variation necklace, but the style changes from classic to eclectic. One strand includes gold-colored potato pearls evenly interrupted by gold ver-meil beads and turquoise nuggets. The second strand breaks the symmetrical pattern with 6-mm garnet beads and an assortment of intricate vermeil beads. Gold-filled 20-gauge wire is used to make the same **Double Strand Clasp** for this piece. A pendant dangles from the center of the garnet strand. One extra-large turquoise bead plus a few more vermeil beads sit on a **Curly Headpin**, which is attached to a **Quadruple Loop Eye**. Finally, a **Basic Eye** attaches the pendant to the center of the second strand.

EXOTICA BRACELET

Break all the rules and flex your creative muscles with this exotic double strand bracelet. Turn your back on the constraints of symmetrical patterns by mixing up tiger's-eye chip beads and carved bone beads. There is no right or wrong way to make this piece, which includes gold-filled wire and incorporates the **Basic Hook** and a **Basic Jump Ring** as the clasp. Simply wrap these chunky beads around your wrist twice, and connect the hook-style clasp. For those bound by conformity, this is the perfect artistic exercise to push you in a new direction. The number of beads will vary because each finished bracelet is a one-of-a-kind piece, but the materials listed below are a guideline for what you will need to complete this project.

Materials

- 8" (20 cm) of 20-gauge (.8 mm) gold-filled round wire

- approximately 7" (17.5 cm) of tiger's-eye chip beads

- assortment of tiger's-eye round beads (4 mm, 6 mm, 8 mm)

- assortment of carved bone beads

- two gold-filled bead tips

- 2' (60 cm) of medium-weight beading wire

- basic tool kit (see page 31)

1. Use the gold-filled wire to make one **Basic Jump Ring** and one **Basic Hook**, and set these aside for later use.

2. Attach a bead tip to one end of the beading wire.

3. Next, begin to string your chip beads and bead assortments in a random pattern so that you have a group of round tiger's-eye beads and some bone beads sandwiched between 1" (2.5 cm) segments of chip beads.

4. Continue stringing your random pattern until you have approximately 14" (35 cm) of beads on your beading wire. (If you normally wear a bracelet that is larger or smaller than 7" [17.5 cm], you will need to alter this accordingly.)

5. Finish the strand with another bead tip.

6. Use round-nosed pliers to curl the bead tip hooks around the **Basic Jump Ring** and the loop on your **Basic Hook**.

Jeweler's Tip:

Before stringing a piece, consider how it will be worn. If it requires flexibility but also needs to be extra strong because of heavy beads, then beading wire is your best option. For a piece that needs to drape or has smaller beads (such as pearls or heishi beads), a softer stringing material, such as nylon or silk, is usually best.

Design Advice:

Try using binder clips (which are normally used for paper) or tape on the ends of your stringing medium as you work on new designs. This way, if you change your mind, you can take off beads or add new beads on either end rather than removing all your beads. Once you finish stringing, hold up the piece for your final approval. Is it long enough? Does it drape well? These are important items to consider before you finish a new piece.

Variation Idea:

If you still want the look of the double strand bracelet but want to tone down its wild appearance without losing the earthy aspect of natural gemstone beads, then consider petite tube-shaped beads, referred to as heishi beads. Although this variation design is much smaller than the original, the electric green of the gaspeite heishi beads can't be missed. To add to the rustic style, the sterling silver **Basic Hook** and **Basic Jump Ring** are slightly textured, which you can easily do by hitting them with a ball peen hammer. Then add a sweet sterling "Love" charm to the jump ring clasp to create a dainty dangle element.

VICTORIANA EARRINGS

Vintage crystal beads immediately denote a feeling of elegance and opulence from the past. The term "vintage" refers to beads made after World War II and up to about 1970. Although vintage beads aren't as old as antique beads, which pre-date World War II, they are still very precious because they are no longer manufactured.

Bead making was one of the original cottage industries. Today, bead suppliers travel throughout Europe to find these sparkling treasures, and it's not unusual for them to discover a stash hidden away in an elderly widow's attic. Due to their rarity, vintage crystals can be more costly than modern-day crystals, but you only need a few to create a brilliant piece of jewelry. With this Victoriana earring design, you just need two vintage crystals and some wire and you'll be able to make a rare, finely crafted piece of jewelry that will dazzle everyone.

Materials

- 15 ¹/₂" (9 cm) of 21-gauge (.72 mm) round sterling wire
- two 6-mm pink vintage bicone crystal beads
- basic tool kit (see page 31)

1. To begin this earring project, you need to use sterling wire to make two of each of your findings, including **Basic Ear Hooks**, **Double Loop Eye Pin**, and **Quadruple Loop Eye**.

2. Once you have these pieces made, string one crystal bead onto your **Double Loop Eye Pin**.

3. Then use the **Wrapped Loop** technique to create a loop at the top of the eye pin, but before wrapping it closed, slip the **Quadruple Loop Eye** component onto the loop.

4. Finally, using flat-nosed pliers, gently open the loop on the ear hook, slip the **Quadruple Loop Eye** component on, and again use flat-nosed pliers to close the ear hook loop.

5. Repeat steps 2 through 4 to assemble your second earring.

Jeweler's Tip:

When shopping for vintage crystals, the bead rule of thumb is truer than ever: "If you see a bead you really want you'd better buy it, or you may never see it again." This isn't always the best advice for your wallet, but it is important in relation to vintage beads because, remember, these are no longer manufactured. Some of the colors, shapes, and cuts are not available in any contemporary equivalent. Once they are gone, they are gone.

Design Advice:

This may sound obvious, but it's important: Remember to make what you like. No matter what's hot or what's not, ultimately, you need to be the person who loves your jewelry the most. Experimentation is great, but don't force yourself to make jewelry that isn't "you" just because it's the latest fashion trend. Listen to your creative voice and be true to yourself, and this will automatically come out in your work.

Variation Idea:

There's nothing wrong with occasionally using purchased findings. When you do, make sure you indulge in Eurowires, also known as leverbacks, for your vintage earrings. This variation design has only two minor differences, yet it illustrates so well how all beads are not equal. For this alternate pair of vintage earrings, Eurowire ear hooks are teamed up with a **Double Loop Eye Pin**; **Quadruple Loop Eye**; and faceted, dark purple vintage crystals. The shape is also different. The original design has a diamond-shaped crystal, referred to as a "bicone" in crystal lingo, but for this pair, the shape is a large oval. The facets on these beads are what really attracts attention.

CELEBRATION NECKLACE

Many jewelry makers find themselves collecting and hoarding lampwork beads, but why keep these miniature artistic artifacts locked away in a bead box? Celebrate them and show them off in spectacular jewelry designs. Instead of worrying about each bead's pattern matching exactly, concentrate on color. Pick out beads with similar color combinations. In this case, red, green, and white are combined in this Celebration lampwork and glass necklace. Solid color spacers and lampwork beads help bring together the different patterns of stripes, flowers, and dots to form a cohesive design. To add another facet to the piece, incorporate lampwork beads into the clasp with the **Triple Loop Beaded Hook** and **Beaded Quadruple Loop Eye**. Exhibit your collection around your neck and receive the ultimate enjoyment from your lampwork beads.

Materials

- 8" (20 cm) of 20-gauge (.8 mm) round sterling wire

- fifteen 12-mm multi-colored red, green, and white lampwork beads in various patterns

- twelve 10-mm red lampwork beads

- fifty-six 4-mm green glass beads

- twenty-six 4-mm red glass beads

- 2' (60 cm) of medium-weight beading wire

- two crimp beads

- basic tool kit (see page 31)

1. Begin by using two 12-mm patterned lampwork beads and 20-gauge (.8 mm) wire to make a **Beaded Quadruple Loop Eye** and a **Triple Loop Beaded Hook**.

2. Thread one end of your beading wire through a crimp bead and the middle loop of either the eye or hook made in the previous step, and then secure the crimp bead.

3. Start stringing on your beads in the following order: one 4-mm green bead, one 4-mm red bead, one 4-mm green bead, one 12-mm patterned lampwork bead, one 4-mm green bead, one 4-mm red bead, one 4-mm green bead, and one 10-mm red lampwork bead.

4. Continue to string on beads in this order until you have used all your beads and have about 15" (37.5 cm) of beads strung.

5. To finish off the necklace, string the end of your beading wire through another crimp bead, then through the middle loop of the other part of your clasp (whichever one you did not use in step 2), and then secure the crimp bead.

Jeweler's Tip:

Before stringing any necklace, lay out the entire design on a bead board first. This way, you can rearrange the beads until you find a pattern you like. Although a bead board isn't a requirement, it can save you a lot of time restringing pieces, and it is also a good tool to help determine how long a piece will be once you finish stringing it.

Design Advice:

Start keeping a sketchbook with design ideas in it. One design idea tends to generate another, and it's a shame to let any of them slip away just because you don't have the time or supplies handy to make them. You don't have to be an accomplished sketch artist. These are for your eyes only. As you start to collect ideas, your designer's sketchbook will eventually become a valuable resource on those days when your muse is silent.

Variation Idea:

The same clasp design, **Triple Loop Beaded Hook** and **Beaded Quadruple Loop Eye**, is included in this two-tone pearl choker. Instead of stringing it on beading wire, use **Wrapped Loops** to connect the pearls, creating a beaded chain of pearls. These silver and white pearls are referred to as "potato" pearls because they are not perfectly round and thus their shape is more potato-like in appearance. The 21-gauge (.71 mm) wire works really well in this piece because it fits through the small holes in the pearl beads, but it is still strong enough for the clasp, which, because of the beads on both the hook and the eye, can hardly be seen, creating a seamless design.

THE FLIRT ANKLET

Link chain enables this "flirty" anklet to adjust in size. The **Basic Hook** easily inserts into the long chain links or in the eye of the attached dangle hematite heart. Sixteen 6-mm hematite beads are suspended from sterling silver **Curly Headpins** and attached evenly down the length of the chain using the **Simple Loop** method. Hematite is a perfect match with sterling silver, and the round hematite beads create a great deal of movement, so the dangles swing as you walk. The extra length of chain doubles as a way to expand or retract the length of the piece and adds an extra detail of interest to the overall design.

Materials

- 1 ½" (3.5 cm) of 20-gauge (.8 mm) round sterling wire
- 3 ½' (1 m) of 21-gauge (.71 mm) round sterling wire
- 9 ½" (24 cm) of long- and short-link sterling chain
- sixteen 8-mm hematite beads
- one hematite heart bead
- basic tool kit (see page 31)

1. First, using the 20-gauge (.8 mm) round sterling wire, make a **Basic Hook** and set this aside for later.

2. Next, use the 21-gauge (.71 mm) round sterling wire and make seventeen **Curly Headpins**.

3. Slip the hematite heart bead onto one of the headpins, and attach it to one end of your chain using the **Wrapped Loop** method.

4. Now, take a moment to study the link pattern of your chain. You'll notice that it is made up of an alternating pattern of one long link and three smaller links.

5. Take the remaining **Curly Headpins**, slip one 6-mm hematite bead onto each one, and using the **Simple Loop** technique, attach each of the sixteen beads and headpins to the center link in the small links section of the chain. If necessary, trim off any excess wire from your headpins and file the ends smooth as you attach each one to the chain.

6. To complete your anklet, attach the loop of the **Basic Hook** you made in step 1 to the end of the chain that is opposite the hematite dangle you made in step 3.

Jeweler's Tip:

When making anklets, it's a good idea to make them as sturdy as possible. Because of their location on the body, they endure a lot more wear and tear than your average piece of jewelry and are more likely to be caught on carpets or bed linen if the wearer isn't careful. How the piece is worn is just as important as how it looks when completed.

Design Advice:

When using wire elements in your designs, consider all your options. A **Basic Eye** is typically used as part of a clasp, connecting to a hook-type component. However, it doesn't always have to fill this same role in your jewelry creations. You can make it part of a chain or add it to an ear hook and attach a dangling bead. By using your wire pieces in unusual ways, you begin to break barriers and invent new design alternatives.

Variation Idea:

Be a little adventurous with this variation on The Flirt, and make your own chain by alternately connecting **Basic Jump Rings** and **Basic Eye** findings. Then attach sherbet-colored dotted lampwork beads and dangle them from the jump rings on whimsical **Curly Headpins**. Finally, finish it off with a **Basic Hook**. To ensure the strength of the nonsoldered chain, this piece is made of 20-gauge (.8 mm) round gold-filled wire. One secret for quickly making your own chain is to work with two pairs of pliers, one in each hand, so you can firmly snap the jump rings closed as you add each component to your design.

CUBISM EARRINGS

Prepare to be noticed whenever you wear these dramatic dangles. The aurora borealis finish (also referred to as AB finish) on the cube-shaped crystal beads demands attention as each bead reflects the light and colors around you. The inclusion of sterling wire and chain enhances the icy nature of the crystals, while the daisy spacer beads add a finishing touch to each dangling bead. Each crystal-and-daisy-bead station rests on top of **Double Loop Eye Pins**. The chain has a dual purpose in this design: connecting eye pins to **Triple Loop Ear Hooks** and creating movement as each of the six strands of beads swing and sway with every turn of your head.

Materials

- 15" (37.5 cm) of 21-gauge (.71 mm) round sterling wire

- six 4-mm clear AB cube-shaped crystal beads

- twelve sterling daisy spacer beads

- approximately 4" (10 cm) of sterling link chain

- basic tool kit (see page 31)

1. First, use the round wire to make six **Double Loop Eye Pins**, and set these aside for later use.

2. You also need to make two **Triple Loop Ear Hooks**, one for each earring, but do not flatten the loops with nylon-nosed pliers at this point. You'll see why soon.

3. Next, cut your pieces of chain. The number of links for each piece is up to you and also depends on the type of chain you use. The chain pattern used for the earrings pictured is made up of three small links alternating with one large link. You need to cut two pieces of chain measuring approximately 3/4" (1.5 cm) and four pieces approximately 1/2" (1 cm) in length.

4. Take one **Double Loop Eye Pin** and slide on one daisy bead, one cube crystal, and another daisy bead.

5. Use round-nosed pliers to make a **Simple Loop** on the end of the eye pin, cutting off excess wire as needed.

6. Repeat steps 4 and 5 until you have beads and loops on all six of the eye pins.

7. Now open the loops at the top of each bead and eye pin component you just made, attach them to the ends of each chain piece, and gently close the loops around the chain links.

8. At this point, you're ready to attach your chain and bead segments to each loop of your **Triple Loop Ear Hook**. Slide the last link of each chain piece onto your ear hooks, snaking the link around the loops until you have one short, one long, and another short chain-and-bead segment on each ear hook loop. (The longest chain segment is in the middle and the shorter ones are on each side of it.)

9. Finish each earring by gently using nylon-nosed pliers to flatten the loops on the ear hooks.

Jeweler's Tip:

Have your polishing cloth nearby when working so you can wipe down your wire a few times before you begin. It takes only a few minutes, and it will make a world of difference with your finished product. If you work a lot with wire, you may want to invest in an ionic jewelry cleaner, which can clean all types of jewelry quickly and safely. This way, as you begin to increase your collection of wire and bead jewelry, you'll always have a way to clean it later.

Design Advice:

Play around once in a while. Children are so inventive and unhindered when it comes to the creative process, and most of this comes from simply playing. They don't have a bunch of preordained rules in their heads and aren't afraid to fail. They just have fun, and from this comes imaginative new ideas. Allow yourself to be a kid again, and don't stress or put requirements on yourself all the time. Remember the reason you began to make jewelry in the first place—because it's fun!

Variation Idea:

Gary Helwig, of www.wigjig.com, used one of his famous wire jigs to create these ear-ring variations. By using a jig, Gary is able to produce precisely matching pieces. For a more classic slant, he selected gold-filled wire and beads to accompany brilliant white pearls. Rather than use the **Triple Loop Ear Hooks** as just ear hooks, Gary added another dimension to this ear hook finding by lengthening the top part of the hook and using it as a combination ear hook and headpin. The result is a long, elegant line.

CRYSTAL CONNECTION EARRINGS

People will be amazed when you tell them that you made all the wire components that are integral elements in this unusual earring design. Only you will know how easy it was as you smile smugly to yourself. Truthfully, although the **Beaded Ear Hooks**, **Triple Loop Eye Pins**, and **Curly Headpins** are central to these long and luscious earrings, the beads play a large part in the overall "wow" affect. First, there is the inclusion of peridot-colored aurora borealis bicone beads. This lighter shade of green continues to increase in popularity as more fashion-forward trend-setters realize its potential with dark colors, such as black and brown, as well as brighter colors, including orange and lemon. Finally, vermeil beads and bead caps, which hug the curly crystal dangles, add a touch of intricate detailing.

Materials

- 14 ½" (36 cm) of 21-gauge (.71 mm) round gold-filled wire

- six 6-mm peridot-colored AB bicone crystal beads

- two 3.5-mm vermeil beads

- four 6-mm vermeil bead caps

- basic tool kit (see page 31)

1. Start by using the gold-filled wire to construct two **Triple Loop Eye Pins** and two **Curly Headpins**.

2. Use more gold-filled wire and two 6-mm peridot-colored crystal beads to make two **Beaded Ear Hooks**.

3. Slide one crystal bead and one 3.5-mm vermeil bead onto one of the **Triple Loop Eye Pins**, and use the **Wrapped Loop** technique to connect the eye pin to the ear hook.

4. Next, take a **Curly Headpin** and add on one vermeil bead cap, one crystal, and another bead cap.

5. Attach the **Curly Headpin** to the middle loop of the **Triple Loop Eye Pin** using the **Wrapped Loop** technique.

6. Repeat steps 3, 4, and 5 to complete your second matching earring.

Jeweler's Tip:

The importance of filing wire cannot be overemphasized. When working with designs that include wire as a primary element, it is really crucial that you file the wire ends as you work. Then, after you are finished, it's a good idea to double-check each section for rough edges or pointy bits of wire. If necessary, gently file any areas that might cut or scratch the wearer. You want your jewelry to look good and feel good as well.

Design Advice:

Every once in a while, you'll come upon a moment when it's time to step away from the bead board. You can't always be in the creative mode. It comes and it goes, but it will eventually return. Just don't try to force it back, or you'll find yourself becoming more frustrated. Go take a walk; watch an old movie; read an endearing Victorian novel. If you feel you must be productive, then clean up your work area or organize your wire and beads. Whatever you do, allow yourself some time off and give your muse a little rest and relaxation when you feel your creative juices have dried up.

Variation Idea:

Gold continues to have plenty of pizzazz in this variation design, which includes beautiful rectangular-shaped freshwater-pearl beads. Highly textured vermeil beads dangle from **Triple Loop Eye Pins** on the end of each earring and are attached using the **Simple Loop** method; the center segments of pearls and crystals are connected using the **Wrapped Loop** technique. Dazzling 4-mm clear aurora borealis crystals decorate the **Beaded Ear Hook** and adorn the center of the earring design on each side of the pearls.

GLAM-PACKED NECKLACE

You can produce instant glamour by incorporating the right beads into your designs. The "bling-bling" of this necklace comes from the dichroic lampwork and aurora borealis crystal beads. Dichroic glass is a high-tech reflective glass containing thin layers of alloys such as titanium and silicon. The technology is more than 100 years old, but dichroic glass has been used in artwork only since the latter part of the twentieth century. Aurora borealis is a reflective finish that encourages light to dance off faceted crystals. These sparkling enhancements are teamed with teal-colored potato pearls, smaller round white pearls, and a **Basic Hook** and **Basic Eye** sterling clasp. The entire necklace is almost completely hand-knotted and measures approximately 26" (65 cm) in length.

Materials

- 6" (15 cm) of 20-gauge (.8 mm) round sterling wire

- fifty-four 6-mm teal-colored potato pearls

- eighteen 4-mm clear AB bicone crystal beads

- ten 4-mm round white pearls

- four 10-mm white and blue mixed dichroic lampwork beads

- four 12-mm white and blue mixed dichroic lampwork beads

- one #4 white carded beading thread (nylon or silk) with attached needle

- two sterling bead tips

- basic tool kit (see page 31)

1. With the 20-gauge (.8 mm) wire, make a **Basic Hook** and a **Basic Eye** for the clasp and set these aside to attach after you have strung your necklace.

2. Remove your beading thread from the card and add a **bead tip** to the end.

3. Using the **Knotting** technique, string on the following beads, knotting between each one: one crystal, two teal-colored pearls, one white pearl, and one crystal.

4. Tie another knot after your last crystal bead, and then string on one teal-colored pearl, one 10-mm dichroic lampwork bead, another teal-colored pearl, and knot after your last bead in this pattern.

5. Repeat the pattern of beads from steps 3 and then step 4.

6. Next, repeat the pattern of beads from step 3 and 4, but this time, use a 12-mm dichroic bead instead of a 10-mm bead. Do this two times.

7. At this point, you are almost at the center of your necklace, and your pattern is going to change just a little as you work your way back up the other side of the necklace. String on the following beads, knotting between each one: one crystal, two teal-colored pearls, one white pearl, two teal-colored pearls, one white pearl, two teal-colored pearls, and one crystal.

8. Continue to create the second half of your necklace using the same patterns from above, but this time you'll begin by alternating with the bead pattern from step 4 and then step 3 because you are creating a mirror image of what you previously strung. Also, make sure that your first two dichroic bead stations include 12-mm beads and your second two dichroic bead stations include 10-mm beads.

9. To complete the necklace, finish the end with your second bead tip, and use round-nosed pliers to attached the **Basic Hook** to one bead tip and the **Basic Eye** to the other.

Jeweler's Tip:

If you don't have a beading awl, try using a corsage pin or a stickpin for your knotting needs. Professionals traditionally use an awl, but these alternative tools can also work in a pinch. Many jewelry-making suppliers also carry a handy tool called the Tri-Cord Knotter, a specialized tool developed for knotting between beads. Both methods (either knotting by hand or with the tool) require practice, but with persistence, you can produce some wonderful results.

Design Advice:

Mull over a design before you finish it. One way to do this is by using multiple bead boards, one for each piece. Arrange the beads and wire components on a board, but don't string them yet. Wait a day or two and then take another look. If inspired, move pieces around or add more. Again, leave it for a time. Let the piece naturally emerge as you think about it in the back of your mind. You'll be surprised at the ideas that can pop up when you don't rush a project.

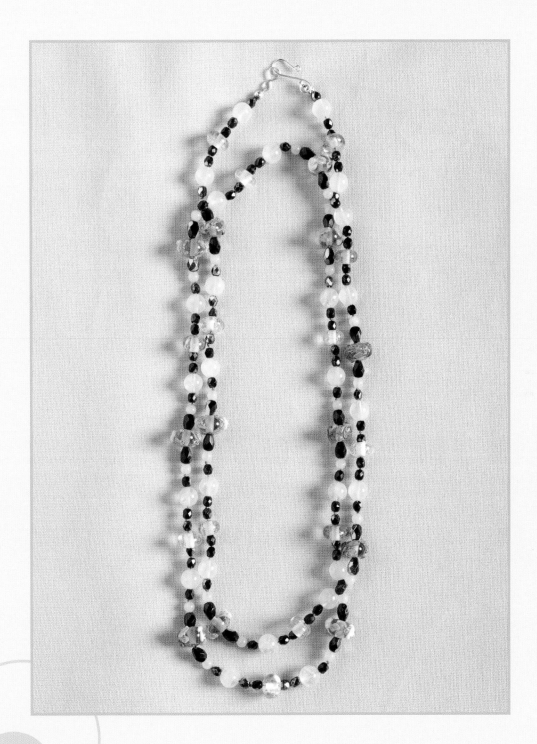

Variation Idea:

Pink dichroic lampwork beads and jet aurora borealis Czech crystals still provide plenty of glamour and glitz for this long, luxurious design, which measures 40" (100 cm), but the color palate is altered. Along with these sparkling embellishments, pastel rose quartz beads and more lampwork beads, this time decorated with dainty pink flowers, make up the rest of this partially hand-knotted necklace. The light hues of pink combined with the dark sparkling crystals produce an elegant contrast. This variation necklace also includes the **Basic Hook** and **Basic Eye** clasp in sterling silver. A long necklace like this can be worn as one long strand (great for shirts with a collar), or double it up to create two 20" (50 cm) strands.

DAISY BRACELET

Quadruple Loop Eye components resemble petite wire flowers in this fun, colorful crystal and wire bracelet. The **Triple Loop Hook** continues the floral theme design as it connects to the last wire "daisy" in the bracelet. The seven bicone crystals, each a different color, alternate with the flower components. If you love color, then this is your chance to mix it up a bit but still create a piece that will fit in with more classic jewelry. Don't worry about matching this bracelet to a particular outfit because it will go with just about everything in your wardrobe.

Materials

- 4' (1.2 m) of 21-gauge (.71 mm) round sterling wire
- one 6-mm ruby red AB bicone crystal bead
- one 6-mm blue zircon AB bicone crystal bead
- one 6-mm fuchsia AB bicone crystal bead
- one 6-mm opal-colored AB bicone crystal bead
- one 6-mm light amethyst AB bicone crystal bead
- one 6-mm emerald green AB bicone crystal bead
- one 6-mm light peach AB bicone crystal bead
- basic tool kit (see page 31)

1. Make one **Triple Loop Hook** and set aside for future use.

2. Make seven **Quadruple Loop Eye** components.

3. Now begin your bead and flower chain by using wire to make a **Wrapped Loop**, but before wrapping the loop closed, slide one **Quadruple Loop Eye** onto the loop.

4. Thread a bead onto the wire, and again begin a **Wrapped Loop**, but before closing it, attach another **Quadruple Loop Eye**.

5. Continue this pattern of alternating **Quadruple Loop Eye** components and beads until you have used all your crystal beads and all your eye components, except when you attach the last bead, instead of an eye component, attach the middle loop of your **Triple Loop Hook** onto the last **Wrapped Loop** before closing it.

Jeweler's Tip:

Some jewelry makers like to use a rawhide hammer to flatten components. This is a good alternative to flattening them with nylon-nosed pliers, and it also helps harden the wire. Just be careful not to overwork the wire when using this method. If you hit it too hard, especially if the wire is thinner than 21-gauge (.71 mm), you can cause too much stress and break the piece.

Design Advice:

For color and design ideas, observe your surroundings. Look for unusual color combinations in wallpaper samples, fabric swatches, or even fine oil paintings. Nature can also provide inspiration. The natural curve of a leaf might lead to a new wire component or a bouquet of flowers might be the perfect color scheme for your next jewelry design.

Variation Idea:

In this bracelet variation, Gary Helwig, from www.wigjig.com, shows how it is possible to make precision wire components by creating them on a wire jig rather than using hand tools. For these two bracelets, he used gold-filled wire and magnetic clasps with an attached safety chain. (The little bit of chain is a great addition because magnetic clasps can sometimes come apart unexpectedly.) Gary also used the **Wrapped Loop** technique to connect beads—jade for one and gold-stone for the other—to **Quadruple Loop Eye** "daisies."

GALLERY OF JEWELRY AND FINDINGS

Janice Parsons, CEO of www.beadshop.com, combined chalcedony tube-shaped beads with frosted blue crystals. A fan of dangles and sterling daisy spacer beads rest on top of sterling **Curly Headpins** and are attached to the center of the necklace using the **Simple Loop** technique. Janice finished the ends of the necklace with crimp beads and two **Basic Jump Rings**, which are attached to strands of matching blue suede. The fan of **Curly Headpins** is reminiscent of the style of ancient Egypt, while the suede ties bring a more contemporary feeling to the finished piece.

Jill Sharp, from Blue Piranha, www.bpjewelry.com, brings the **Basic Jump Ring** to a whole new level in this gold-filled wire and garnet chain maille bracelet, which feels as luxurious as it looks. Jill used a multitude of gold-filled jump rings to create a complex wire flower design, and she repeated this flower pattern throughout the bracelet. In between each flower, she connected 4-mm garnet beads and tiny gold-filled accent beads using the **Simple Loop** technique. She finished off the piece with a variation of the **Basic Hook**.

The focus of this necklace, created by Jenny Zhou from www.beadshop.com, is a yummy oval-shaped watermelon tourmaline bead. Dangling from a **Curly Headpin** using a **Simple Loop**, the bead is attached to a small chain of alternating **Basic Jump Rings** and **Basic Eyes**. Jenny used sterling wire to create her centerpiece, and then soldered her jump rings closed. Matching suede is attached to the last ring of the chain, which she then finished off with another **Basic Jump Ring** and a **Basic Hook** variation.

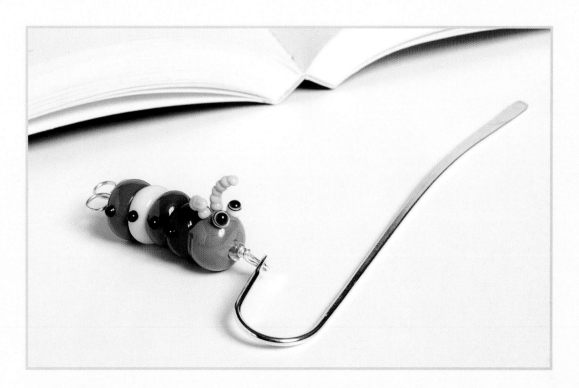

Glass artist Daphne "D.D." Hess, www.members.tripod.com/ddhess, used unique wire findings to accent her lampwork beads. Her whimsical lampwork bookworm hangs from a metal bookmarker on a **Triple Loop Headpin** and is attached using the **Wrapped Loop** technique. In her bracelet, D.D. connected her signature floral lampwork beads with "flower" **Quadruple Loop Eye** components. Her clasp includes a variation of the **Beaded Hook** and **Basic Eye**. She used the **Wrapped Loop** technique again in this piece to connect each wire flower to each flower bead. The flower details on her beads are a perfect match with her wire flower components.

Jennifer Shibona's metal clay bead was the inspiration for this beaded necklace, designed by Tammy Powley. Jennifer made the centerpiece using metal clay, which she formed, textured, and fired to create a focal bead made of fine silver. A pattern of butterflies and sunbursts make up the relief pattern scattered across the surface of the bead. Tammy then used wire and Jennifer's bead to make a **Beaded Loop Eye**. The necklace's five strands are an asymmetrical mixture of Japanese glass seed beads; Czech, Austrian, and vintage crystals; and various shapes and shades of natural amethyst. The ends of the multistrand necklace are attached to Jennifer's bead using a **Basic Hook** and a **Basic Eye**.

Amy Hardy is a jewelry designer from Fire Mountain Gems and Beads, www.firemoun taingems.com. She created two pieces especially for the gallery. For her sterling silver malachite cabochon ring, Amy used inspiration from the **Triple Loop Headpin** and **Curly Headpin** to create a triple loop accent and curly wire accent on each side of the band. In her Swarovski crystal bracelet, she connected brightly colored crystal cube beads with **Wrapped Loops**, **Quadruple Loop Eye** components, and a variety of other wire pieces. She finished the bracelet with a tiny bicone crystal dangling from a **Curly Headpin** and a **Basic Hook**.

Sandy "Ruby" Fischer, from Ruby's Jewelry Designs and Beadwork, www.rubysbead work.com, demonstrates the power of beads and unique wire findings in this gold-tone wire and faux-pearl set. Ruby used the following findings techniques to design the chain and centerpiece for the necklace: **Quadruple Loop Eye**, **Basic Jump Ring**, **Beaded Loop Eye**, **Triple Loop Eye Pin**, **Basic Eye**, and **Triple Loop Hook**. She connected all the findings and beads using the **Simple Loop** technique. The **Triple Loop Ear Hooks** with tiny pearl accent beads complete the set.

Gary L. Helwig, from www.wigjig.com, used his wire jig skills to make three pairs of gold-filled wire and gemstone bead earrings. For each of his goldstone earrings, he strung two 8-mm goldstone beads and tiny gold-filled accent beads onto a long **Triple Loop Ear Hook** so that the hook also acts as a headpin. He used a similar design for his jade earrings, though this time he included two gold-filled beads on each side of the gemstone bead. In his onyx earrings, Gary dangled **Quadruple Loop Eye** components from chain, and then used the **Wrapped Loop** technique to add three onyx dangles on each earring.

Iris Sandkühler is a highly skilled jewelry artist and the Director of e-Learning for www. beadshop.com. This two-toned necklace, designed and constructed by Iris, mixes sterling metal plate with gold-filled wire. She used a series of **Basic Eye** components linked together for her chain and then completed the chain with a larger **Basic Eye** and a **Basic Hook**. On the pendant, Iris soldered curls of wire, similar to a **Curly Headpin**, onto a round piece of sterling plate. To attach the chain to the pendant, she pierced the plate and used a variation of the **Curly Headpin** and **Wrapped Loop** technique. As a final accent, Iris has an additional curly component piece secured to the bottom of her pendant.

Rhona Farber, of Over the Moon Jewelry, www.overthemoonjewelry.com, calls this bracelet and earring set "Ocean," because the colors remind her of the sea. For the earrings, Rhona used sterling **Triple Loop Headpins** and **Wrapped Loops** to secure large oval, opal-colored glass beads to Eurowire ear hooks. Petite 4-mm pearls dangle from loop of the headpins. Rhona's bracelet incorporates the **Double Strand Clasp** and more **Wrapped Loops** to connect alternating segments of pearls and faceted crystal beads in pastel shades of blues and greens.

Vicky X. Nguyen is a jewelry artist and the purchasing and inventory manager for www.beadshop.com. She combined a unique assortment of wire findings and beads in these two earring designs. Her hoop earrings are long and dramatic, but the use of tiny **Curly Headpins**, pearls, crystals, and small-link chain also make them soft and feminine. The bold red crystal earrings she created use a variation of the **Basic Ear Hook** that then continues into a teardrop shape, from which Vicky used the **Simple Loop** technique and more **Curly Headpins** to dangle ruby red bicone crystal beads.

Sandy "Ruby" Fischer, from Ruby's Jewelry Designs and Beadwork, used silver Artistic Wire to accent these unusual purple fiber-optic beads for this earring and bracelet set. Crystal, glass, fiber-optic beads, and silver bead caps dangle from the **Triple Loop Eye Pin** on each earring. Ruby then connected each earring piece to Eurowires using the **Simple Loop** method. For her bracelet, she used **Quadruple Loop Eyes**, **Basic Jump Rings**, and variations of the **Beaded Loop Eye** and the **Triple Loop Hook**.

SUPPLIERS

The following companies generously donated the supplies used for creating the jewelry projects in this book:

Beadshop.com

158 University Avenue
Palo Alto, CA 94301
USA
Phone: 650.328.7925
Email: webmanager@beadshop.com
Website: www.beadshop.com

Beadshop.com is the website of The Bead Shop, which also has a storefront in Palo Alto, California. They offer a huge selection of exceptional quality beads, findings, and tools. In addition to supplies, Janice and her talented team of in-house designers make their own jewelry kits; distribute multimedia classes through DVD, CD, and video; and provide on-site classes in a wide variety of jewelry techniques, from metalsmithing to beading.

Daphne D. Hess Handcrafted Beads

Hobe Sound, Florida
USA
Phone: 772.546.8960
Email: hess9033@bellsouth.net
Website: http://members.tripod.com/ddhess/

This glass artist specializes in flame-worked glass, beads, and jewelry. You can purchase her lampwork beads wholesale or retail through her website or give her a call to find out how she can develop a line of beads for your specific needs.

WigJig

P.O. Box 5124
Gaithersburg, MD 20882
USA
Phone: 800.579.WIRE
Email: custsrv@wigjig.com
Website: www.wigjig.com

WigJig is probably best known for its numerous wire jigs that allow you to create your own wire jewelry components and findings. They also sell a variety of supplies, including beads, wire, tools, findings, hard-copy and web books, CDs, and videos for jewelry makers. Their website offers a way to shop online as well as many pages of free jewelry tutorials covering a wide range of wire- and bead-related techniques.

Additional Resources

USA

MonsterSlayer
Phone: 505.598.5322
Website: www.monsterslayer.com
Metal findings, wire, and beads

ArtgemsInc.com
Phone: 480.545.6009
Website: www.artgemsinc.com
Beads, findings, and jewelry-related supplies

Auntie's Beads
Phone: 866.262.3237
Website: www.auntiesbeads.com
Beads and general jewelry-making supplies

Beadbox
Phone: 800.232.3269
Website: www.beadlovers.com
Beads and general jewelry-making supplies

The Bead Warehouse
Phone: 301.565.0487
Website: www.thebeadwarehouse.com
Stone beads and general jewelry-making supplies

CGM
Phone: 800.426.5246
Website: www.cgmfindings.com
Metal findings, wire, and beads

Fire Mountain Gems and Beads
Phone: 800.355.2137
Website: www.firemountaingems.com
Beads, wire, tools, and jewelry-related supplies

Pure Beads
Phone: 718.458.7602
Website: www.purebeads.com
Specializing in crystal beads from the Czech Republic

Rio Grande
Phone: 800.545.6566
Website: www.riogrande.com
Equipment, beads, metal, and other jewelry-related supplies

Shipwreck Beads
Phone: 800.950.4232
Website: www.shipwreck-beads.com
General jewelry-making supplies

Soft Flex Company
Phone: 707.938.3539
Website: www.softflextm.com
Soft Flex beading wire and general jewelry-making supplies

South Pacific Wholesale Co.
Phone: 800.338.2162
Website: www.beading.com
Stone beads and general jewelry-making supplies

Urban Maille Chain Works
Phone: 303.838.7432
Website: www.urbanmaille.com/
Prefabricated jump rings in all diameters and gauges, kits, and tools

Wire-Sculpture.com
Phone: 877.636.0600
Website: http://wire-sculpture.com/
Wire and general jewelry-making supplies

INTERNATIONAL

The Bead Company of Australia

Phone: 61.2.9546.4923
Website: www.beadcompany.com.au
Beads and general jewelry-making supplies

BeadFX

Phone: 877.473.2323
Website: www.beadfx.com
Canadian supplier of glass, crystal, and seed beads

Beadgems

Phone: 0121.778.6314
Website: www.beadgems.com
UK supplier of beads and jewelry-making supplies

The Bead Shop

Phone: 0127.374.0770
Mail order: 0127.374.0777
Website: www.beadsunlimited.co.uk
UK supplier of beads and related supplies

Canadian Beading Supply

Phone: 800.291.6668
Website: www.canbead.com
Wholesale and retail bead and jewelry supplier

Hobbycraft

(Stores throughout the UK)
Phone: 0120.259.6100
Bead shop and jewelry-making supplier

The House of Orange

Phone: 250.544.0127
Website: www.houseoforange.biz
Canadian supplier of beads and jewelry-related supplies

Katie's Treasures

Phone: 61.2.4956.3435
Website: www.katiestreasures.com.au
Australian supplier of beads and jewelry-related supplies

Kernowcraft Rocks and Gems Limited

Phone: 0187.257.3888
Website: www.kernowcraft.com
UK gem and mineral supplier

Manchester Minerals

Phone: 0161.480.5095
Website: www.gemcraft.co.uk
UK gem and mineral supplier

Mee Ngai Wah in Sham Shui Po

Tel: 86.20.81713226
Fax: 86.20.81713312
Wholesale and retail jewelry supplies from Hong Kong

Spacetrader Beads

Phone: 61.3.9534.6867
Website: www.spacetrader.com.au
Australian supplier of beads and jewelry-related supplies

ABOUT THE AUTHOR

Tammy Powley is a writer and mixed-media artist. She is the author of *Making Designer Gemstone and Pearl Jewelry* and has been the Internet Guide for the About.com Jewelry Making website at http://jewelrymaking.about.com since 1998. Tammy has been published in various print publications, including *Jewelry Crafts Magazine*, *Bead Step-by-Step*, *Art Jewelry*, and *Kid's Step-by-Step*. In addition to studying a large variety of jewelry techniques, from beading to metalsmithing, she has worked extensively with glass, fiber, and paper art. After spending eight years on the art show circuit, she eventually turned to writing about art, though she continues to sell her work through special commissions and galleries. Tammy currently resides in Port St. Lucie, Florida, with her husband, Michael, and a house full of dogs and cats.

ACKNOWLEDGMENTS

To develop and produce a book like this, it takes the help and guidance of many special people, and I could not have completed it or enjoyed the process as much without the invaluable assistance of my friends and coworkers.

First, I want to thank the crew at Rockport Publishers for offering me another opportunity to write and create jewelry, two of my passions. Although there are many people behind the scenes (editors, designers, proofreaders, a photographer, and illustrator to name a few), of special notice are Mary Ann Hall and Betsy Gammons. Both have been there for me whenever I had a question or needed assistance, and that was often!

Judy Love's talent is also an integral part of this creative process. Her wonderful drawings really helped me explain the "how-to" procedures and made this book a step above many other jewelry-making books on the market.

Then there are the suppliers who have generously donated materials, advice, and support throughout the many months that it took to put this book together: Janice Parsons of beadshop.com, Suzanne and Gary Helwig of www.wigjig.com, and lampwork artist D.D. Hess.

The talented jewelry artists whose work is displayed in the gallery pages are also a group I'd like to thank. To see them take my ideas and turn them into unique jewelry designs was truly inspirational.

Then, of course, there is my husband, Michael. No matter how many late nights I'm up at the computer or at my workbench, Michael is understanding and supportive of the crazy schedule that a book requires of me.